EDITED BY
COLLIN HANSEN

OUR
SECULAR
AGE

TEN YEARS OF READING AND
APPLYING CHARLES TAYLOR

TGC

Our Secular Age: Ten Years of Reading and Applying Charles Taylor

Copyright © 2017 by The Gospel Coalition

Published by The Gospel Coalition
2065 Half Day Road
Deerfield, Illinois 60015

Cover design: Peter Voth
Typesetting: Ryan Leichty

Printed in the United States of America

ISBN: 978-0692919996

ENDORSEMENTS

"As Christians, we sometimes misunderstand not only the answers our secular neighbors have but the questions they are asking too. No philosopher has offered more insight regarding the state of belief in the modern age than Charles Taylor. In *Our Secular Age*, first-rate evangelical scholars and practitioners deliver 13 essays in which they explore and apply Taylor's thought. This work will benefit all Christians by teaching them to communicate the gospel to a secular culture with neither ignorance nor fear."

RUSSELL MOORE, president, Ethics & Religious Liberty Commission of the Southern Baptist Convention

"To be secular, says philosopher Charles Taylor, is to have no final goals beyond this-worldly human flourishing. This is only one of the many insights from which pastors can profit from Taylor's work in their ministry of the gospel to an age that has substituted spirituality and authenticity for religion and doctrine. The essays in this helpful volume do more than borrow from Taylor: they engage, question, develop, and occasionally criticize his influential account of our complex cultural moment in which we all—moderns and postmoderns, millennials and non-millennials—are trying to live, move, and have our being as disciples of Jesus Christ. Reading and applying the insights of those who have read and applied Taylor is a salutary exercise in understanding oneself and others in an age that is not only secular, but fragile, frustrated, and confused."

KEVIN J. VANHOOZER, research professor of systematic theology, Trinity Evangelical Divinity School

"Charles Taylor's *A Secular Age* is a landmark book, and the essays collected here ponder it intelligently and charitably. Some echo Taylor, some extend his ideas, some contest his claims, but all engage his argument with a seriousness that the book deserves—and that Christ's church needs."

ALAN JACOBS, distinguished professor of humanities in the honors program at Baylor University and author of *How to Think: A Survival Guide for a World at Odds*

"Easily one of the best books I've read this year. Here is wisdom from Taylor, received with appreciation and appropriate criticism, with application for Christians on mission in North America in the 21st century."

TREVIN WAX, Bible and reference publisher at B&H, author of *This Is Our Time: Everyday Myths In Light of the Gospel*

"The 'social imaginary,' the 'buffered self,' and the 'immanent frame'—these Charles Taylor neologisms and more are illuminated and expounded (and critiqued) in this helpful collection of essays, shedding light on aspects of our present age, from theology to politics and from art and to medicine. After reading these chapters, I was compelled to do two things: (1) I revised the sermon I was to preach the next day, and (2) I went online and ordered *A Secular Age*. I want to know more!"

BILL KYNES (PhD, Cambridge), senior pastor of Cornerstone Evangelical Free Church, Annandale, Virginia

"Though this book will help you to understand, appreciate, and critically engage with Charles Taylor, that's not its real benefit. Read it mainly for a dozen fascinating conversations about a different area of the church's life, and learning how to better engage our culture in our present secular age."

JONATHAN LEEMAN, editorial director, 9Marks

CONTRIBUTORS

BRUCE RILEY ASHFORD serves as provost and professor of theology and culture at Southeastern Baptist Theological Seminary. He co-authored *One Nation Under God: A Christian Hope for American Politics* and is the author of *Every Square Inch: An Introduction to Cultural Engagement for Christians*. You can follow him at *www.BruceAshford.net*.

MIKE COSPER is director of The Harbor Institute for Faith and Culture in Louisville, Kentucky. He is the author of *The Stories We Tell: How TV and Movies Long for and Echo the Truth, Rhythms of Grace: How the Church's Worship Tells the Story of the Gospel*, and co-author of *Faithmapping: A Gospel Atlas for Your Spiritual Journey*.

BOB CUTILLO, MD, is an associate faculty at Denver Seminary, where he teaches on health and culture; an assistant clinical professor in the department of family medicine at the University of Colorado School of Medicine; and a physician at Colorado Coalition for the Homeless. He has worked for many years in faith-based health care for the uninsured and under-served.

GREG FORSTER (PhD, Yale University) is the director of the Oikonomia Network, a visiting assistant professor of faith and culture at Trinity International University, and the author of numerous books and articles.

COLLIN HANSEN serves as editorial director for The Gospel Coalition. He is the author of several books, including *Young, Restless, Reformed: A Journalist's Journey With the New Calvinists*. He previously worked as an associate editor for *Christianity Today* magazine, edited *Revisiting 'Faithful Presence'*: To Change the World *Five Years Later*, co-edited *Four Views on the Spectrum of Evangelicalism*, and co-edits the Cultural Renewal series with Tim Keller.

MICHAEL HORTON is the J. Gresham Machen professor of systematic theology and apologetics at Westminster Seminary California. His books include *Putting Amazing Back into Grace, Christless Christianity*, and *The Gospel-Driven Life.*

BRETT MCCRACKEN is a senior editor for The Gospel Coalition and pastor in Southern California. He is the author of *Hipster Christianity* and *Gray Matters*, and his most recent book is *Uncomfortable: The Awkward and Essential Challenge of Christian Community.*

JEN POLLOCK MICHEL is the author of *Keeping Place: Reflections on the Meaning of Home* and *Teach Us to Want: Longing, Ambition and the Life of Faith.* She also regularly contributes to *Christianity Today*'s Her.meneutics blog and *Today in the Word*, a devotional publication of Moody Bible Institute. She lives in Toronto with her family

ALAN NOBLE is co-founder and editor-in-chief of Christ and Pop Culture and an assistant professor of English at Oklahoma Baptist University. He received his PhD from Baylor in 2013.

DEREK RISHMAWY is a systematic theology PhD student at Trinity Evangelical Divinity School. He is a columnist at *Christianity Today* and writes at his own blog, *Reformedish*. He co-hosts the *Mere Fidelity* podcast.

ALASTAIR ROBERTS (PhD, Durham University) writes in the areas of biblical theology and ethics, but frequently trespasses beyond these bounds. He participates in the *Mere Fidelity* podcast and blogs at *Alastair's Adversaria.*

JOHN STARKE is lead pastor at Apostles Church Uptown in New York City.

CARL TRUEMAN (PhD, Aberdeen) is the William E. Simon visiting fellow in religion and public life at Princeton University. He has written more than a dozen books, and co-edits with Bruce Gordon the *Oxford Handbook of Calvin and Calvinism*.

TABLE OF CONTENTS

1

HOPE IN OUR SECULAR AGE

COLLIN HANSEN

It wasn't the first time a young evangelical woman had lamented to me the aimless, rebellious character of her younger brother. Growing up together their home had tended toward the fundamentalist end of the Protestant spectrum. Church was mandatory; doubt was discouraged. In college and afterward she found her way into an evangelical congregation that tended toward Reformed theology. But her younger brother never seemed to grow up. He deliberately antagonized his parents and sister.

She described to me one scene in particular that typified his protest. While gathered together in the living room, as the rest of the family watched television or read a magazine, her brother flaunted his copy of a Richard Dawkins screed against religion. Only he didn't seem to be actually reading the book. Rather, he peered over the pages to see what kind of reaction he was inciting.

Classic case of a "subtraction story," I told her. A what? The term comes from the 2007 book *A Secular Age* by the Catholic philosopher Charles Taylor. Her brother probably couldn't explain any sophisticated scientific or philosophical objections to Christianity. But he found in Dawkins a "hero narrative" to explain his "coming of age," his maturation away from the childish religion of his youth and family.[1]

"The core of the subtraction story consists in this," Taylor writes in A Secular Age, "that we only needed to get these perverse and illusory condemnations off our back, and the value of ordinary human desire shines out, in its true nature, as it has always been."[2]

Fundamentalism could not protect this young man from the forces of modernity that make faith increasingly implausible. Indeed, an intellectually restrictive fundamentalism might have even made his reaction more likely, because as Taylor observes, the "more childish one's faith, the easier the flip-over."[3]

Evangelical apologists have traditionally responded with biblical proofs and technical counterpoints to scientific materialism as popularized in the last decade-plus by the so-called New Atheists, including Dawkins. But what if science, reason, and logic aren't the problem or solution to firm faith? What if the challenge runs far deeper?

What if the problem of our secular age is more fundamental?

NOTHING MORE FORMATIVE

Probably no book published in the last 10 years has been so formative for my thinking and ministry as Taylor's A Secular Age. Taylor (b. 1931) challenges my own faith as much as he

---

1   Charles Taylor, A Secular Age (Cambridge, MA: The Belknap Press of Harvard University Press, 2007), 365.

2   Ibid., 253.

3   Ibid., 307.

equips me to counsel other believers swimming upstream in cultures not conducive to belief. I regret that the length of his work (nearly 900 pages) and the density of his prose preclude most pastors and other Christian leaders from even picking up the book. Yet I remain convinced that taking up the challenge of Taylor would equip Christians with invaluable historical, theological, sociological, and philosophical context as they carry out the Great Commission (Matt. 28:18–20) in our secular age. Pastors, missionaries, and social workers in particular would benefit.

"In fact, these are the core audience for this book precisely because I believe Taylor's analysis can help pastors and church planters understand better the contexts in which they proclaim the gospel," writes James K. A. Smith, who teaches philosophy at Calvin College. Probably no author has done more than Smith to popularize Taylor for the benefit of the church. "In many ways, Taylor's *Secular Age* amounts to a cultural anthropology for urban mission."[4]

The purpose of this book, then, is to read and apply Taylor to various aspects of the church's life and mission. Interpreters and practitioners will assess Taylor from multiple perspectives, including his reading of the Reformation and medieval philosophy, and apply *A Secular Age* to everything from healthcare to liturgy to pop culture and politics. In this introduction I aim to familiarize readers, many of whom will never pick up *A Secular Age*, with Taylor's basic arguments and also with a key interpreter from the last decade. And I seek to demonstrate one particular way Taylor has deepened my understanding as a writer, parent, and church leader.

---

4   James K. A. Smith, *How (Not) to Be Secular: Reading Charles Taylor* (Grand Rapids, MI: Eerdmans, 2014), xi.

WE'RE ALL THOMAS NOW

Nothing is easy about faith in a secular age.

"Faith is fraught, confession is haunted by an inescapable sense of its contestability," Smith writes. "We don't believe instead of doubting; we believe *while* doubting. We're all Thomas now."[5]

Religion in a secular age is a private affair. That's why the courts, media, and other cultural gatekeepers respond with incredulity when believers claim constitutional protection for their right to practice religion in the public square. Especially before the 16th-century Reformation but for a long time afterward, religion had been commonly known as a collective practice with communal accountability for the sake of the whole. Conformity was necessary.

"In a world of indigence and insecurity, of perpetually threatening death, the rules of family and community seemed the only guarantee of survival," Taylor writes. "Modern modes of individualism seemed a luxury, a dangerous indulgence."[6]

Today, though, religion is the luxury, the dangerous indulgence. Faith is now more difficult than unbelief. We're adrift in stormy seas of doubt—every man, woman, and child fighting for the lifeboat of belief. Something fundamental has shifted in Western culture that runs deeper than outward changes in technology. So what happened? That's the question Taylor seeks to answer.

"How did we move from a condition where, in Christendom, people lived naively within a theistic construal, to one in which we all shunt between two stances, in which every-

---

5   Smith, *How (Not) to Be Secular*, 4.
6   Taylor, *A Secular Age*, 168.

one's construal shows up as such; and in which moreover, unbelief has become for many the major default option?"[7]

The world has changed. And religion changed with it.

GOD AS GOD

Less than one year after Taylor published *A Secular Age*, I published *Young, Restless, Reformed: A Journalist's Journey with the New Calvinists*.[8] In this book I sought to describe an unexpected shift in the beliefs and practices of young evangelicals. At the same time that moralistic therapeutic deism came to be known as the default religion of American teenagers,[9] a significant minority of evangelicals had gone looking for an older, more countercultural theology. They found it in Calvinism.

In travels around the United States I asked young and old, lay and clergy, "Why?" I'll never forget one pastor who answered, "Because it's true." Granted, I said, but why would it suddenly be popular after a steady decline since at least the early 1800s?[10] I published the book without a sufficient answer. But Taylor helped me find that answer—and a warning.

Taylor provides historical and philosophical explanations for what Christian Smith and his colleagues with the National Study of Youth and Religion have revealed in their research. The decreasing numbers of Western youth who practice religion are indoctrinated into a version that empha-

---

7   Taylor, *A Secular Age*, 14.

8   Collin Hansen, *Young, Restless, Reformed: A Journalist's Journey with the New Calvinists* (Wheaton, IL: 2008).

9   See Christian Smith with Melinda Lundquist Denton, *Soul Searching: The Religious and Spiritual Lives of American Teenagers* (New York, NY: Oxford), 2005.

10 See Nathan O. Hatch, *The Democratization of American Christianity* (New Haven, CT: Yale, 1989), 171.

sizes God as distant and uninvolved, though concerned with our good behavior. Mostly he just wants us to be happy. Religion aims to give us what we want, in material or therapeutic terms. Of course, that's not how the Bible portrays God or how Christians have historically understood him.

The key theological question for our secular age, then, is this: Does God get to be God? The answer, even for many self-described Christians, is, "No, only on our terms." You'll see many young adults who grew up in evangelical churches try to argue that unless we recast biblical and historical notions of God, we'll lose the next generations. And for them that ultimatum makes sense. In our secular age they couldn't possibly hold on to orthodox faith. A God who is not for us, they say, cannot be against us. As Taylor says of these arguments in *A Secular Age*, the turn to self has fundamentally reconfigured Christianity:

> And hence what was for a long time and remains for many the heart of Christian piety and devotion: love and gratitude at the suffering and sacrifice of Christ, seems incomprehensible, or even repellant and frightening to many. To celebrate such a terrible act of violence as a crucifixion, to make this the centre of your religion, you have to be sick; you have to be perversely attached to self-mutilation, because it assuages your self-hatred, or calms your fears of healthy self-affirmation. You are elevating self-punishment, which liberating humanism wants to banish as a pathology to the rank of the numinous.[11]

---

11   Taylor, *A Secular Age*, 650.

I mentioned that Taylor helped me answer, "Why Reformed theology today?" Here's how: You really only have two options in a secular age. Either God is for you, on your own terms, or God sets the terms. And Reformed theology, with doctrines such as unconditional election, revels in the triune God as transcendent and inscrutable, yet immanent and sympathetic. God is no mere cosmic butler. To read about a God who doesn't merely cater to our whims, you'll need help from theologians of earlier generations. At least for a growing minority of young evangelicals, 18th-century Reformed theologian Jonathan Edwards is still their homeboy, more than 10 years later.[12]

"This is what makes Jonathan Edwards not only unthinkable but reprehensible to modern sensibilities: Edwards's God is *about God*, not us."[13]

APOLOGETIC HOPE

Calvinism would not be gaining popularity in our secular age, though, if it were merely counterculture. You can't just turn back the clock to 16th-century Geneva or 18th-century Massachusetts. The conditions of belief have changed. To see Taylor applied today, you need to visit Timothy Keller in his thoroughly secular Manhattan context.

Compared to our ancestors, we have a bigger problem with evil and suffering. They lamented evil and suffering— and they experienced more of it than we do. Meanwhile, we demand answers from God and engage in theodicy. Why do

---

12   Collin Hansen, "Young, Restless, Reformed: Calvinism Is Making a Comeback—And Shaking up the Church," *Christianity Today* (September 2006): 32–38.

13   Smith, *How (Not) to Be Secular*, 115.

we, unlike our ancestors, believe the existence of evil could disprove God?

"Ancient people did not assume that the human mind had enough wisdom to sit in judgment on how an infinite God was disposing of things," Keller explains in his most recent apologetic work, *Making Sense of God*, a title Taylor would surely note with interest.[14] Taylor describes how the same philosophy that gave us modern medicine also gave us modern skepticism:

> The great invention of the West was that of an imma-nent order in Nature, whose working could be system-atically understood and explained on its own terms, leaving open the question whether this whole order had a deeper significance, and whether, if it did, we should infer a transcendent Creator beyond it.[15]

Given these conditions, Keller aims to give modern skeptics a reason for God.[16] And Keller's apologetic approach closely resembles Taylor's. Smith describes Taylor's apologetic in three steps. First, level the playing field with secularists by pointing out the problems faced on both sides. Second, show how "immanentist" accounts fall short of solving the problem in an emotionally and intellectually satisfying manner. Third, reveal how Christians might better explain human experi-ence.[17] Compare that approach to Keller's three-step process:

---

14   Timothy Keller, *Making Sense of God: An Invitation to the Skepti-cal* (New York, NY: Viking, 2016), 37.

15   Taylor, *A Secular Age*, 15.

16   See Timothy Keller, *The Reason for God: Belief in an Age of Skepti-cism* (New York, NY: Viking, 2008).

17   Smith, *How (Not) to Be Secular*, 120.

enter the culture, challenge the culture, and then appeal to the culture.[18]

Unless you read all the way through *A Secular Age*, you may get the impression that Taylor sees little hope for the future of Christianity. But he and Keller both see a limit to how much longer secularists can demonize the religion of our Western inheritance. Because as religion goes away, evil does not, contrary to the projections of Dawkins and his cohort. And secular hopes for universal justice and benevolence can't be built on a mere "subtraction theory."[19] The more we expect of others, the more they will disappoint us, Taylor argues: "Our age makes higher demands of solidarity and benevolence on people today than ever before."[20] It's not sustainable. God continues to haunt this secular age with our desire for goodness. Taylor writes:

> Our age is very far from settling in to a comfortable unbelief. Although many individuals do so, and more still seem to on the outside, the unrest continues to surface. Could it ever be otherwise? The secular age is schizophrenic, or better, deeply cross-pressured. People seem at a safe distance from religion; and yet they are very moved to know that there are dedicated believers. . . . It's as though many people who don't want to follow want nevertheless to hear the message of Christ, want it to be proclaimed out there.[21]

---

18   Timothy Keller, *Center Church: Doing Balanced, Gospel-Centered Ministry in Your City* (Grand Rapids, MI: Zondervan, 2012), 120.
19   Taylor, *A Secular Age*, 576.
20   Ibid., 695.
21   Ibid., 727.

Take heart, church. But beware. Taylor sees trouble in our camp.

ONE MORE COPING MECHANISM?

While many Reformed readers have read Taylor with profit, that doesn't mean he necessarily sympathizes with their project. Further chapters will examine his critique more closely. To summarize, Taylor faults the Protestant Reformation and modern evangelical Christianity for disenchanting the world and turning the focus on the self rather than on God through shared religious rituals.[22] He laments the shift from embodied to intellectual faith in what he calls Reform, described by Smith as "Taylor's umbrella term for a variety of late medieval and early modern movements that were trying to deal with the tension between the requirements of eternal life and the demands of domestic life."[23]

I wouldn't expect a practicing Roman Catholic like Taylor to commend the Reformation. And there's no doubt the Reformation unleashed a torrent of practices and beliefs that the magisterial Reformers did and would condemn. If nothing else Taylor helpfully corrects believers in both Geneva and also Rome when he says, "Perhaps there is no 'golden age' of Christianity."[24] So even as I object to Taylor's critique, I want to hear him out. And with Taylor's help, we see a major problem ahead for the young, restless, Reformed.

The "restless" component of the moniker has attracted the most attention in the last decade, and for good reason. It doesn't seem to fit when juxtaposed with "Reformed." But

---

22   Taylor, *A Secular Age*, 774.
23   Smith, *How (Not) to Be Secular*, 142.
24   Taylor, *A Secular Age*, 745.

that's the point. Writing in 2007 I didn't know how things would shake out. Taylor captures why the "God as God" theology of Edwards and modern apologetics of Keller would appeal to many young evangelicals trying to buck a secular age. At the same time, Taylor showed me why Reformed theology would offer an enticing "coming of age" story for youth who grew up in pragmatic or liberal congregations. Something like the young man reading Dawkins, reading Edwards became for some of them a convenient, even safe way to create an individual identity apart from their parents and home church. But might their own children in our secular age rebel in yet another direction? We don't yet know, then, whether the children of the "young, restless, Reformed" will imbibe more of the *restless* or the *Reformed*.

Has the preaching of their churches and teaching of their parents weaned them off a need for individual authenticity?

Or has Reformed theology become just one more tool for coping with our secular age?

TEST OF FAITH

That's no abstract question. It is a test of genuine faith. If pure, undefiled religion is about God and not just our own flourishing, then it will lead us "to visit orphans and widows in their affliction, and to keep oneself unstained from the world" (Jas. 1:27). Where you see holiness, sacrifice, and love, you see religion that delights in God, religion that can survive a secular age. Edwards would say these are sure signs of religious affection. In our modern language, they're signs that we're following the risen Christ and not just treating our therapeutic needs.

Whether he recognizes it or not, Taylor aligns with at least one key aspect of the evangelical tradition. The Reformation may have risked anarchy and secularism, but it did so in search of this pure religion. Evangelical renewal movements have been seeking the same thing ever since. And not even Taylor seems willing to turn back that clock:

> If ours tends to multiply somewhat shallow and undemanding spiritual options, we shouldn't forget the spiritual costs of various kinds of forced conformity: hypocrisy, spiritual stultification, inner revolt against the Gospel, the confusion of faith and power, and even worse. Even if we had a choice, I'm not sure we wouldn't be wiser to stick with the present dispensation.[25]

Yes, we risk succumbing to faddish theological trends. Yes, we struggle to escape the self. Yes, we need a more embodied religion to hold us accountable.

But after 10 years of reading and applying Taylor, I'm confident.

There is hope in our secular age.

---

25   Taylor, *A Secular Age*, 513.

TAYLOR'S COMPLEX, INCOMPLETE HISTORICAL NARRATIVE

CARL TRUEMAN

Postmodernism famously proclaimed the death of all master narratives (except, of course, that one). Taylor is no postmodernist in that sense, but he knows history is complicated, and that any account of how we have arrived at our present state requires the interweaving of multiple narratives. Thus, as he set himself the task of answering the question of why it was almost impossible not to believe in God in 1500 and yet an easy, perhaps even the easiest, option in 2000, he assumed a task of massive and multifarious historical complexity.

In approaching this topic, what Taylor does is historically interesting. Master narratives may be dead, but most people still think in terms of simple, straightforward accounts of why religion is in such trouble. Darwin proved we came from the apes. Science has disproved religion. Religion is responsible for most of the world's ills. And so on. From the (relatively) sophisticated accounts offered by such as Richard Dawkins and Christopher Hitchens to the rather more concise but floridly expressed versions offered by Manhattan taxi drivers, these simple stories grip the imagination like so many metaphysical soap opera plot lines. Taylor shatters such simplistic myths, demonstrating that secularity as a concept is complicated—and so is the elaborate pathway by which it has emerged.

The strands of Taylor's overall narrative are easy to identify. From a Reformation-Protestant perspective, perhaps the most serious claim is that he sees the rise of voluntarism and nominalism in the late Middle Ages as laying the foundation for shifting from a world that naturally carries its own rich meaning(s) to one where human beings create such meaning for themselves.[26]

The Reformation, as early fruit of nominalism/voluntarism, plays a central role in the narrative. By abolishing the traditional hierarchical distinction between the sacred and the secular, and thereby sanctifying the ordinary, it performed a twofold service. First, it released Christendom from the monopoly of Rome by offering an alternative (soon to become many alternatives). Second, by making the secular

---

26   *Voluntarism* is the term given to the theological position that emphasizes the logical priority of God's will over his intellect, as opposed to intellectualism, which asserts the priority of his intellect over his will. Put simply, intellectualists argue that God wills something because it is good, while voluntarists argue that something is good because God first wills it. *Nominalism* in the late medieval period referred to the view that words construct reality rather than refer to or reflect reality. For the nominalist, then, Rex and Fido are both dogs because they each have more in common with each other than with, say, a block of stone or a tree, and not because they both possess some universal "doggy" essence. The implication of both positions is to shift thinking away from reality as independent and external and toward that of a linguistic construct.

sacred it inadvertently created a context where the sacred could ultimately become secular.

The first point is uncontestable. The Reformation did shatter the religious unity of Western Europe and did ultimately make religious commitment a matter of choice rather than of geographical birthplace. The idea of "choosing" a church remains a profoundly Protestant idea, one that is confusing to traditional Roman Catholics.

The second is more contentious but historically arguable. The move from Michelangelo's Sistine Chapel to Vermeer's Milkmaid does not signal a lost sense of the sacred. Yet God did become more distant in the late 17th and early 18th century. Voluntarism had injected arbitrariness into the relation between God and his creation (at least from the perspective of the human knowing subject) and this shift eventually fueled Deism. Deism in turn attenuated God's role to that of creator and maintainer of order. In such a scheme, a personal God—indeed, God in any traditional form—became unnecessary.

In a world like this, the sense of the sacred that suffused such paintings as those of Vermeer rapidly vanished, to be replaced either by the merely prosaic or a quest to find the transcendent elsewhere, in the sublime or in nature, which we find in the paintings of Caspar David Friedrich and the poetic philosophy articulated in (and exemplified by) *Lyrical Ballads* of Wordsworth and Coleridge. In such a world, traditional religion remained an option, if increasingly implausible.

Alongside this narrative runs Taylor's account of the changing understanding of the human self. The move here is from what he describes as the porous self to the buffered self.

Building on his earlier masterpiece, *Sources of the Self*[27], Taylor maps out a narrative whereby the medieval self, inhabiting a world full of fairies and demons and supernatural powers, was more integrated with his physical (and thus spiritual) environment. In one thought-provoking passage, he points out that black bile was not thought to cause melancholy but was actually believed to *be* melancholy. The sharp distinction between the physical and the spiritual simply did not exist in the way that later generations understood it.

Late-medieval voluntarism and the Reformation to which it gave birth shattered this porous self. Again, it is hard to argue with this narrative. For example, while Taylor doesn't address this fine point, it is well established that voluntarism and nominalism weakened the connection between grace and the sacraments and also between intrinsic reality and divine declarations about what constitutes reality. This shift provided the background to the Reformers' reorientation of theology from sacraments to Word and from justification as divine transformation to justification as divine declaration. The physical and the corporate gave way to the doctrinal and the individual.

While Taylor studiously avoids questions of absolute or transcendent truth, he regards most human beings as unwilling—even unable—to accept that the world is meaningless. Human beings are always seeking to find some meaning in life, even if that meaning is purely immanent.

This search manifests itself in various ways, from the attempts to reconstruct morality on Enlightenment premises (Kant), to build a moral philosophy on the basis of aesthetics (Schiller), to rescue religion from its cultured despisers

---

27   Charles Taylor, *Sources of the Self: The Making of the Modern Identity* (Cambridge, MA: Harvard University Press, 1999).

(Schleiermacher), and to offer a heroic account of human beings in the context of the absurd (Camus). Such drives towards transcendence characterize the cross-pressures Taylor sees as undermining the standard "subtraction" narratives of secularization, whereby science simply displaces more and more of the ground traditionally occupied by religion. The subtraction narrative simply can't make sense of the world. If it did, the world would surely be getting simpler. In fact, it is becoming more complicated.

STORY NEEDS SUPPLEMENTING

Taylor's narrative is vast and complicated and presses into the immediate past, seeing the context for the highly psychologized notions of self with which we all now operate and which mark this present age in profound ways. Taylor makes the obvious connections between Romanticism, especially Schiller, and the later psychoanalytic turn of Freud, followed by Marcuse, who fused the Romantic, the Freudian, and the Marxist in a heady political manifesto for the '68ers. He also argues that the sexual revolution needs to be understood as more than hedonistic libertarianism (of which, say, Hugh Hefner and *Playboy* would be examples). The revolution also arises from the cross-currents of a world wrestling with the "excarnate" impulses of Western thought rooted in voluntarism and Reformation Protestantism, yet striving for a wholeness that does justice to embodied existence.

There are, however, gaps in a number of areas. In saying so, I'm not claiming that Taylor's argument/narrative is not cogent—it is—but that the story needs supplementing.

Perhaps the most obvious lacuna is the explanation of how elite ideas came to shape the social imaginary of ordinary people. This is always going to be a difficult question to answer, because most people do not leave behind written records that reflect on how their thinking has been shaped. And Taylor certainly points to a number of specific factors that had an effect beyond the rarified tomes of the intellectuals. The reformers' attack on the traditional church calendar and their fear of things such as "carnival" flattened time and thereby reshaped ordinary experience of the world. Then there were catastrophic moments such as the French and American Revolutions, the First and Second World Wars, Vietnam, and 9/11. The aftereffects of these events profoundly affected the popular imagination, and Taylor acknowledges them all.

Material factors do not form a major part of Taylor's narrative, yet they are surely vital to understanding the developments he describes. No printing press, no Protestant Reformation, for example. Further, there is much evidence of growing unease with the medieval church in many parts and in many strata of European society, which paved the way for transformed notions of authority in the Reformation apart from the influence of voluntarism. Luther's early successes were in no small part due to the remarkable alliance of nobles, knights, merchants, and peasants who backed his cause against the church.

Ordinary life in the early 16th century wasn't simply trundling on as normal, to be shattered by an intellectual crisis. The rise of cities had transformed the world, from depopulating the countryside to restructuring family and community life. In addition, the rise of production economies put pressure on the old agrarian calendar. Discipline and order were deeply rooted in social and economic changes, not simply in emerging philosophies of time or in breaking the religious monopoly of medieval Catholicism.

Technology too is a critical material factor in the rise of modernity. Technology in and of itself brings with it a certain ontology. It carries with it a sense of control, of power, of the ability to manipulate the world and overcome nature. This perspective connects neatly to Taylor's important distinction between *mimesis* and *poiesis*, which he deals with primarily in terms of a philosophical shift. But that philosophical shift was also connected to a technological shift, and a focus on the latter might help to further explain how the modern social imaginary built upon it came to be so powerful at all levels of society.

We could give numerous examples, from the advent of crop irrigation and fertilizers to the development of the birth-control pill. All such things carry notions of power and control and surely reinforce what Taylor calls the buffered self. Only when sex is detached from social consequences can it become mere recreation, and that change can be attributed as much to contraceptive technology as to anything else.

Think of the advent of the automobile. The arrival of relatively cheap and readily available transport transforms the world, collapsing geography and opening up vistas of possibilities for individuals. If Protestantism gave the Western world religious choice, that choice was still severely limited until relatively recently. Scholarly work on church discipline in places as different as rural Scotland and urban Geneva has indicated the effectiveness of the church in exerting power (and thus restricting choice) when a population is relatively static. Perhaps it is not so much Luther who created religious choice at a practical level but Henry Ford? That is hyperbole, but the question is worth asking. Material conditions are crucial for how the self is constituted and understood.

At no point in history has this point been more obvious than today. Mass media and information technology have transformed the way people think, feeding a consumerist mentality, emphasizing aesthetics, even mainstreaming pornography, which breaks down sexual taboos and commodifies people. Now, it is certainly true that Twitter, Facebook, and smartphones have emerged since Taylor published *A Secular Age*, but they didn't emerge from a vacuum. Movies and television fueled the entertainment industry. They were, and are, critical components in forming the modern understanding of the self. They must feature in any narrative that seeks to explain how and why the ideas of the intellectual elite come to shape the social imaginary as a whole.

A key figure in that story is Edward Bernays, nephew of Freud and the man who deployed his uncle's theories in the area of mass marketing, becoming the founder of modern advertising and PR in the process. His genius was to sell products on the basis of desire, not function: Smoke a cigarette because it makes you look powerful; buy a car because it makes you sexy. Bernays as much as anyone is an architect of this secular age, given that argument now counts for so little on ethical matters, and aesthetics plays such a key role. He's also one vital bridge between the elite and the masses. Bernays helped make a world where the same individuals who never darken the door of a church because they are suspicious of authority will line up for days outside of an Apple store to pay an exorbitant sum of money for a minor upgrade to the device they already possess. The absence Bernays from *A Secular Age*, along with any major discussion of commercialized popular culture, is a significant gap.

NOT YET OVER

Given the pressure now coming against traditional religion on moral and aesthetic grounds—not so much that it is nonsense as it embodies values and promotes behavior regarded as harmful to society—the key issues of our secular age appear to be those of the psychologized self as focused on sexual identity. Taylor's *A Secular Age* is an extremely important contribution into understanding how this situation has come about. Christians need to understand that the dramatic changes we are witnessing in the West are the fruit of a long and complicated history. Any responses we offer must take full account of this complexity.

In closing, however, I must make one more critical comment on Taylor. He's careful throughout to avoid asking about the truth of the ideas he discusses. That is appropriate as his task is descriptive and explanatory. Yet I wonder if a narrative as broad and grand as he offers can ultimately avoid that question. Why do some ideas end up as part of the social imaginary while others do not? We can answer in part by examining the material conditions and processes of cultural development, as suggested above. But even then the nagging question of truth comes back in: If we reject a reductive materialism and believe that material conditions do not strictly determine which ideas flourish and which die out, then why does Idea X win and not Idea Y? Is it merely time and chance, or are certain ideas inevitably more attractive, and if so, why? And can that question be answered purely in terms of describing the processes themselves?

Augustine and Pascal would have an answer: The ultimate dynamic driving this secular age is the denial of our creatureliness and the assertion of our autonomy. The psychological self is the latest stage, allowing us to claim that we are who we think we are and to repudiate all forms of external authority—even that of our own bodies. The story Taylor tells in *A Secular Age* is not yet over, and the next phase is likely to be most traumatic. Human nature isn't a psychological or even a merely social construct. And our constant efforts to deny that truth can only end in disaster.

THE ENDURING POWER OF THE CHRISTIAN STORY: REFORMATION THEOLOGY FOR A SECULAR AGE

MICHAEL HORTON

When the plague spread across England between 1348 and 1350, the Church of England called for periods of intense prayer and fasting. But in the 1990s, in response to the HIV/AIDS crisis, the Church of England called for more government funding for medical research.[28] We tend to think that shifts like this derive merely from explicit intellectual attacks on a "Judeo-Christian worldview," but even those of us who do affirm orthodox Christianity divide inwardly between praying for our daily bread and knowing that it's always there at the grocery store.

It is not merely that our beliefs have changed, but that our way of believing has shifted away from assuming a world

---

28 Steve Bruce, *Secularization: In Defence of An Unfashionable Theory* (New York, NY: Oxford University Press, 2011), 44.

"with devils filled" but where God is our "mighty fortress."
Now we must become masters of our own destiny, keeping
danger at bay by our own collective and calculative reasoning. Even if God plays a role, it is a supporting one, helping us
to achieve "our best life now."

There are too many fruitful pathways in Charles Taylor's *A Secular Age* to engage meaningfully from a theological
perspective in this limited space. And most of those pathways
aren't only spot-on but also stinging indictments of our own
complicities. Unfortunately, this essay will not focus on these
sage insights but on questions of a more critical nature, particularly in relation to my own theological presuppositions
and commitments.

APOLOGETIC FOR CHRISTIANITY OR SECULARITY?

There are many reasons why pastors, especially conservative
Calvinists, should read *A Secular Age*. We tend to think that
what we believe determines how we live. Ideas have consequences, as Richard Weaver put it.[29] True, but consequences
also have ideas. Taylor's embeddedness in the continental
tradition of philosophy (especially Georg Hegel and the
phenomenological tradition of Edmund Husserl and Martin
Heidegger) offers a refreshing alternative to the standard
accounts of secularism that dominate conservative Christian
reading lists. We feel his descriptions in our gut because he's
describing *our* world, where we feel and experience the world
differently regardless of focal beliefs.

---

29 Richard Weaver, *Ideas Have Consequences* (Chicago, IL: Univer-
    sity of Chicago Press, 1948; repr. 2013). Interestingly, the bad
    idea he had especially in mind was nominalism, anticipating
    John Milbank's thesis.

At the same time, I wonder if *A Secular Age* overcorrects the intellectualist tendency by embracing a Romanticism in which myths and rituals attain a quasi-independent efficacy. In other words, has Taylor himself lost confidence in the power of the Christian story—including its systematic truth claims (doctrine)—to determine and invigorate our practices?

Taylor is a practicing Roman Catholic who hasn't shied away from bringing his personal convictions to bear on his scholarship.[30] However, *A Secular Age* reveals a complex and perhaps even contradictory set of theological assumptions. On one hand, he's critical of the processes that have disengaged, disenchanted, disembedded, and buffered the self toward an exclusive humanism in which human flourishing is the only goal and immanence the only frame. On the other hand, it is not clear the extent to which his own ideal is specifically Christian.[31]

Taylor shares misgivings about traditional Christianity in ways that suggest he feels personally the attraction of the very trends he explores. In Taylor's view, Christianity is more a set of rituals and behaviors than a system of doctrine, so he

---

30 See for example his 1996 lecture, published as *A Catholic Modernity: Charles Taylor's Marianist Award Lecture, with Responses by William M. She, Rosemary Luling Haughton, George Marsden, and Jean Bethke Elshtain*, ed. James L. Heft (New York, NY: Oxford University Press, 1999). The same can be said of his *Sources of the Self: The Making of the Modern Identity* (Cambridge, MA: Harvard University Press, 1989), which prepared the ground in many ways for *A Secular Age*.

31 His invocation of Matteo Ricci in *A Catholic Modernity* already suggested that Taylor is sympathetic to accommodating the Christian faith to culture. The famous 16th-century Jesuit missionary to China is a controversial figure because of the degree to which he indulged a syncretistic blending of Christianity with native religion.

seems quite comfortable with a syncretistic Middle Ages as his historical analogue to how we should be at home in secular modernity yet with an openness to transcendence.

Taylor hardly avoids doctrine, but many of his most direct normative excurses display an almost visceral reaction against traditional teachings. Eschewing attributes traditionally ascribed to God, Taylor compares God to an expert tennis player;[32] Calvin and Janssen are the only advocates of "a Total Plan."[33] Then he goes on to deny impassibility and immutability, misidentifying the former with "non-emotion," then pitting these classical attributes against the Cappadocian fathers' idea of "person,"[34] as if the fathers saw the same contradiction—much less questioned for a moment God's immutability and aseity. Under the guise of preferring Eastern Orthodox theosis to Western emphases, Taylor frequently abandons his disciplined method in favor of rather emotional and ill-informed reactions against traditional doctrines. Ransom theory is preferable to judicial-penal—the latter at the heart of Catholic and Calvinist conceptions, with "their common hyper-Augustinian roots."[35] He refers to the "hyper-Augustinian doctrines of human depravity, and the inability to escape it without efficacious grace,"[36] in spite of the fact that these aren't "hyper-Augustinian" at all, but simply the sort of run-of-the-mill Augustinianism that you find in Aquinas. This is true even of Calvin's interpretation of predestination, which added nothing new to typical Thomist treatments.

---

32   Taylor, *A Secular Age*, 277.
33   Ibid., 278.
34   Ibid., 278–79.
35   Ibid., 652.
36   Ibid., 511.

On one hand, Pelagianism plays a large role in the march toward "exclusive humanism." On the other hand, the cure (counter-Pelagian movements like the Reformation) was apparently worse than the disease. Wherever the Reformation did not contribute directly to secularization, it did so by provoking a reaction against its emphasis on God's glory and grace, as in the Arminian reaction against "predestinarian orthodoxy." Taylor writes, "This development was inevitable, in view of the very success of Calvinism in changing people's lives."[37] But again, if Calvinism was so concerned with God's glory, above and beyond human flourishing, then how can Taylor's following characterization not be at the same time a lament for the waning of Calvinism's influence?

> We no longer see the pursuit of [human flourishing] as a way of following God, let alone glorifying him. And secondly, the power to pursue it is no longer something that we receive from God, but is a purely human capacity. But as a consequence of this double movement towards immanence, a new concept of human flourishing is born, which is in some ways without precedent. The new understanding is frequently expressed in terms of "nature," following the philosophical tradition which comes down to us from the ancients.[38]

One might naturally conclude that, according to this narrative, Calvinism *lost*, but in Taylor's telling the Reformation is responsible even for secularizing backlashes against it.

In fact, Taylor expresses his gratitude for some of the very secularizing trends he has seemingly criticized:

---

37   Taylor, *A Secular Age*, 84.
38   Ibid.

> If I speak from out of this religious understanding, in
> which I place myself, then this modern turn has brought
> some positive benefits; in say, detaching our view of the
> first mystery (original sin) from an obsessive sense of
> human depravity; and in giving us a distance from the
> judicial-penal view of the atonement.[39]

He's also quite impressed with René Girard's criticism of
the scapegoat mechanism applied to atonement theologies.
Suffice it to say that Taylor doesn't like penal substitution
any more than did Albrecht Ritschl, and for many of the
same reasons.

Further, "Hell, the ultimate separation from God, must
remain a possibility for human freedom, but all the presump-
tuous certainty that it is inhabited must be abandoned."[40]
Notice how the only good reason for hell is protecting human
flourishing (freedom), not God's justice, righteousness,
goodness, and holiness. Is this not indebted to the anthro-
pocentrism at the heart of exclusive humanism that Taylor
otherwise dissects with such skill? To see hell as actually
populated, he asserts, serves our delight in cheering on the
demise of our neighbors (which of course makes belief in
hell inherently sadistic). "Hence the endorsement of sacred
massacres. Modern universalism, 'the decline of Hell,' has
knocked out this prop, and *this seems to be a gain*."[41]

> We can notice, running through much of the Enlight-
> enment a motif of anger at, even hatred of orthodox
> Christianity. . . . What made Christianity particularly

---

39   Taylor, *A Secular Age*, 653.
40   Ibid., 656.
41   Ibid., 671 (emphasis added).

repulsive to the Enlightenment mind was the whole
juridical-penal way in which the doctrine of original sin and the atonement were cast during the high
middle ages and the Reformation. . . . There were some
repugnant aspects of this just in itself. But it became
connected to two doctrines which were potentially
deeply offensive. The first was the belief that only a
few are saved. The second was the doctrine of predestination, which seemed to be generated inevitably from
a belief in divine omnipotence in the context of the
juridical-penal model.[42]

But why wasn't there a massive revulsion against these
doctrines when they were so clearly taught by medieval
scholastics? The Reformers' teaching on *justification* was the
truly novel element. In fact, medieval doctrine at its Augus-
tinian-Thomistic best pressed original sin, double predestination, and a highly penal system, but one in which the satisfaction of God's wrath was dealt with by penance rather than
free justification.

As for "salvation of only a few," that teaching was found
in Aquinas as well as late medieval nominalists like Ock-
ham and especially Biel, who wanted to stress the urgency
of tipping the scales in your favor. The reformers, including
Calvin, emphasized the wideness of God's electing grace.

Nevertheless, Taylor suggests that, recoiling from such
doctrines, there was a general movement away from belief
in hell and the rise of universalism. Even Calvinists began to
reject predestination and to embrace "confidence in the human power to do good," including the power of reason, which

---

42   Taylor, *A Secular Age*, 262.

undermined mystery and authority until science is seen as refuting religion.[43]

In short, whatever Taylor disagrees with doctrinally becomes a candidate for contributing to exclusive humanism. If the doctrine didn't actually play a direct (though perhaps unwitting) role in encouraging secularization, then it promulgated theses so abhorrent to the modern mind that it provoked exclusive humanism as a legitimate reaction. Calvinism is blamed even for erstwhile Calvinists abandoning it in the direction of exclusive humanism.

Yet again Taylor appears to vacillate. On the one hand, "the juridical-penal model" is obsessed with "the dark side of creation." On the other hand:

> Simply negating it, *as many of us modern Christians are tempted to do*, leaves a vacuum. Or it leaves rather an unbelievably benign picture, which cannot but provoke people either to unbelief, or to a return to this hyper-Augustinian mode of faith, *unless it leads to a recovery of the mystery of the Crucifixion, of world-healing through the suffering of the God-man*. Certainly this central mystery of Christian faith becomes invisible, if one tries to paint the dark out of Creation.[44]

Here we have the clearest expression of Taylor's own theological solution: to navigate the Scylla of "hyper-Augustinian" (i.e., traditional medieval and Reformation beliefs) and the Charybdis of nihilism via the middle course of an ostensibly more incarnational paradigm emphasized by distinctly

---

43   Taylor, *A Secular Age*, 262.
44   Ibid., 319 (emphasis added).

modern appropriations of an Eastern Orthodox soteriology.
He continues:

> Modern humanism tends to develop a notion of hu-
> man flourishing which has no place for death. Death
> is simply the negation, the ultimate negation, of flour-
> ishing; it must be combated, and held off till the very
> last moment.[45]

Taylor himself seems stranded between *wanting* to negate
these doctrines and yet worrying that the only alternative is
nihilism. It is understandable that people think that orthodox Christianity is passé—even impossible. He writes, "From
here it would be easy to take the step that orthodox, com-
munion-defined Christianity really belongs to an earlier age;
that it makes little sense, and is hard to sustain today."[46] It is
hard to know how much Taylor agrees with in the modernist
reaction and the extent to which he too thinks that much of
traditional Christian teaching "belongs to an earlier age."

It is not only with respect to particular doctrines but the
emphasis on doctrine itself where Taylor finds modernism's
anti-dogmatism compelling. Long before the Reformation,
Western Christianity has been too obsessed with a rational
system, he argues. Again, there is something important to
this observation, which has characterized Eastern critiques of
Latin theology. However, there's also a modernist (especially
Romantic) streak running throughout these contentions,
as Matthew Rose suggests. Noting similarities to modernist
presuppositions ("deeds, not creeds," faith as a subjective
leap and "a spirituality of transforming love" set over against

---

45   Taylor, *A Secular Age*, 320.
46   Ibid., 289.

knowledge of God), Rose sees *A Secular Age* less as an apologetic for Christianity than for Christian accommodation to our secular age.[47]

TAYLOR'S TAKE ON THE REFORMATION

Taylor admires a broadly participatory folk religion. In Buddhist and Christian civilizations, he says, there have been "radical renouncers" and also "those who go on living within the forms of life aiming at ordinary flourishing, while trying to accumulate 'merit' for a future life." For them, Christianity was not specific beliefs as much as a way of life based on ritual practices: creeping to the cross, invoking saints to help with the process of salvation, basically trying to remain in a state of grace without being a 100-percenter. There were always others—especially the monks and nuns—who would go over and beyond, but "this distinction was radically 'deconstructed' in the Protestant Reformation, with what fateful results for our story here we are all in some way aware, even though the task of tracing its connections to modern secularism is still very far from completed."[48]

In contrast, the Catholic Reformation stressed "minimal conformity to the demands of God: the avoidance of mortal sin, or at least doing whatever is necessary to have these sins remitted. What emerges from all this is what we might call 'moralism,' that is, the crucial importance given to a certain code in our spiritual lives." He concedes, "This is perhaps not an outlook which it is easy to square with a reading of

---

47   Matthew Rose, "Tayloring Christianity." *First Things* (December 2014): 25–30. https://www.firstthings.com/article/2014/12/tayloring-christianity.

48   Taylor, *A Secular Age*, 18.

the New Testament, but it nevertheless achieved a kind of hegemony across broad reaches of the Christian church in the modern era."[49]

I wonder, what counts as secularization here? Cambridge historian Patrick Collinson observed that the Reformation was "an episode of re-christianization or even primary Christianization" that interrupted "a process of secularization with much deeper roots."[50] But in Taylor's account, the Reformation spurred secularization in countless ways, even though the resulting exclusive humanism that he exegetes so compellingly looks a lot like the seeds of medieval semi-Pelagianism and syncretism (not to mention Renaissance Pelagianism and pantheism) come to full flower.

Strikingly, Taylor doesn't lay the blame for desacralization at the feet of the Reformation war on idols and superstition. In this regard, the Reformation is simply the culmination of the Axial revolution that began with the Hebrew prophets, putting an end to "paganism and polytheism," which results in "disenchantment, the end of a cosmos of spirits respondent to humans, and the coming of an impersonal order defined by the moral code."[51]

So does Taylor think that the Bible itself is the problem and the Reformation was simply returning to the inherent problems of Judeo-Christian anti-paganism? I think he does: "To draw on this power, you have to leap out of the field of magic altogether, and throw yourself on the power of God

---

49   Taylor, *A Secular Age*, 497.
50   Patrick Collinson, *The Religion of Protestants: The Church in English Society 1559-1625* (Oxford: Clarendon, 1982), 199.
51   Taylor, *A Secular* Age, 364. The concept of an "Axial revolution" is itself controversial. Originating with Karl Jaspers's *The Origin and Goal of History* (trans. Michael Bullock; London: Routledge, Keegan and Paul, 1953) and mediated especially

alone. This 'disenchanting' move is implicit in the tradition of Judaism, and later Christianity."[52] His fascinating exploration of "higher and lower times," with "Feasts of Misrule" as necessary counter-balances to everyday order (for example, Carnival before Lent) tends toward a valorization of a relatively paganized Christian culture.

Whereas the 15th-century Council of Constance organized a network of temporary brothels for the holy synod, and prostitution was generally tolerated as "a sensible prophylactic against adultery and rape, with all their disruptive consequences," laws were passed in Lutheran and Reformed territories to close them down. And while "there was an aura of sanctity around poverty," in England and Holland especially widespread attempts were made to rehabilitate beggars, teaching them a trade.[53]

It becomes clear, then, that Taylor's problem isn't just with the Reformation but with the "anti-sacred" movement rooted in the Bible itself. Even if the Protestant rage for order got out of control, it is hard to imagine that the reformers' concerns—and effectiveness in actual reforms—with respect

---

by Max Weber (see Arpad Szakolczai, *The Genesis of Modernity* (London: Routledge, 2002), 80-81), the thesis has been challenged by Iain Provan, *Convenient Myths: The Axial Age, Dark Green Religion, and the World that Never Was* (Waco, TX: Baylor University Press, 2013). Oxford historian Diarmaid MacCulloch described it as "a baggy monster, which tries to bundle up all sorts of diversities over four very different civilisations, only two of which had much contact with each other during the six centuries that (after adjustments) he eventually singled out, between 800 and 200 BCE" ("The Axis of Goodness," *The Guardian* [March 17, 2006]).

52   Taylor, *A Secular Age*, 74.
53   Ibid., 106-09.

to church and family contributed to secularization more than the creeping of the cross, Carnival, and a degenerate clergy. Taylor seems to pine for the day when the average Christian lived in a world that was more a matter of things you do than of explicit convictions: deeds, not creeds. And even here, the morality that he commends appears to favor the Dionysian spirit of paganism to what he at least characterizes as the more Apollonian spirit of the prophets and the New Testament.

Again, I'm left wondering if Taylor's ideal is a Neoplatonic cosmology with a thin veneer of Christian rituals and symbolic practices. Regardless, his working assumptions are shaped significantly by Max Weber and Radical Orthodoxy (especially John Milbank).[54]

CAN WE MOVE ON?

Steve Bruce provides fresh and (to my mind incontrovertible) proof for the thesis that wherever the process of modernization (i.e., industrialization, technology, individualism,

---

54   Taylor gives several nods to Milbank's narrative in this work, acknowledging its formative role in his overall project. This has become the working assumption in recent anti-Reformation polemics (e.g., Brad Gregory, David Bentley Hart, Hans Boersma, Peter Leithart, and a host of others). We cannot here pursue the many problems with these controversial theses about the Reformation's relation to disenchantment and the school of nominalism. But they have no basis in the sources and have been subjected to withering critique by specialists at every key point. Indeed, it was at the Council of Trent where nominalism triumphed, while Lutheran and Reformed scholastics explicitly rejected nominalism and generally affirmed Aquinas on the relevant points of dispute.

rationalization, education, rights, and economic and political liberalism) takes root, secularization inevitably follows.[55] I'm more inclined to this neo-secularization thesis than most other Christians, including Taylor. Yet the thesis pertains to cultures and societies. It lacks any criteria or methods that could determine whether Christ's kingdom will prevail, even in the West once more. As Abraham examined the empirical realities, he had no reason to believe he'd be a father at all—much less the father of a nation and, ultimately, of a worldwide family. God's promise trumped the data. "When the Son of Man comes, will he find faith on the earth?" (Luke 18:8). Jesus answers his question with the promise, "I will build my church and the gates of hell will not prevail against it" (Matt. 16:18).

Even if Taylor's narrative can be contested at various points, it reminds us how much of secularization is internal. It advances rarely by external opposition but by a gradual process of assimilating the Christian drama, doctrines, doxology, and discipleship to the nihilistic plots of this fading age. The ultimate threat is never that the world will continue to be worldly, reducing reality to human flourishing and the immanent frame, but that churches will fail in their calling to re-narrate human existence and deliver Christ to a needy world through the means of grace—that Christians will surrender merely their souls or minds to Christ while giving their bodies to the powers and principalities of this present evil age. God's speech in judgment and grace wages war against autonomous individualism and self-crafting.

The Reformation could have happened only because everyone assumed a porous cosmos in which our lives now

---

55   Steve Bruce, *Secularization: In Defence of An Unfashionable Theory* (Oxford: Oxford University Press, 2011).

mattered because of a final judgment and eternity. Luther's
search for a gracious God made sense in a world terrified
by evil, death, and hell. But how does the gospel even make
sense in a cosmos where human flourishing is the only end,
God's majesty is reduced to benign empowerment for our
life projects, and hell is a depressed state of mind? There may
be "transcendence" *within* this world, including ourselves.
A baseball game or a ballet performance may bristle with
intimations of the sacred. Cresting the summit of a glisten-
ing granite peak may fill you with an overwhelming sense of
the sublime. Joining a march may charge your soul with the
exhilaration of being part of something larger than yourself,
the arc of history that bends toward justice.

But these are all quasi-mystical moments *within* time,
nature, history, and the self, rather than the *in-breaking* of
eternity into time. Such events may trigger a new consciousness of the always-and-everywhere "miracle" of nature, but
there is little expectation of a personal God intervening in
history, showing up on our doorstep to do a new thing. The
sense of a genuinely transcendent God, qualitatively distinct
from creation and yet the one in whom we live and move and
have our being, is waning if not eclipsed by secular liturgies
that reduce the horizon of desire to what we can access with
a smart phone.

Consequently, we can move on as if the question of
justification, much less the arcane debates surrounding it,
mattered to the average person today. Or can we? Interestingly, Nietzsche linked denial of God to guilt. When
Zarathustra, the prophet of Antichrist, beheld "the ugliest
man," he at first turned away in horror but succumbed to
the plea for a hearing. Why did you kill God, Zarathustra
demanded? "He always saw *me*: I desired to take revenge on
such a witness—or cease to live myself. The god who saw
everything, *even man*: this god had to die! Man could not *en-*

dure that such a witness should live. Thus spoke the ugliest man." Zarathustra's horror turned to admiration, since "only the doer lives." "How poor is man (he thought in his heart), how ugly, how croaking, how full of secret shame. . . . Alas, was *he* the Higher Man whose cry I heard? I love the great despisers."[56] Robert J. Lifton, a psychologist and pioneer in brain research, observes that the source of many anxieties and indeed neuroses in society today is a nagging sense of guilt without knowing its source.[57]

It is hard to imagine an imaginary frame in which the intervention of a redeeming Creator-God could be more relevant than in its violent clash with the buffered self. The professionals may call it *ennui* or alienation, but where does it come from? Isn't it too deep to be attributed to the circumstances of our time and place and to be remedied by superficial solutions?

In any case, surely it is a sign that the nihilists are wrong that we can even have spirited debates about the mystery of existence. And exposing (rather than catering to) the self defined by Augustine as radically "turned-in-on-itself" remains the greatest mission and privilege of gospel ministry.

---

56   Friedrich Nietzsche, "The Ugliest Man" in *Thus Spoke Zarathustra*, trans. Thomas Common (London: Pantianos Classics, 2016), 203.

57   Robert J. Lifton, "The Protean Style," in *The Truth About the Truth*, ed. Walter Truett Anderson (New York, NY: Tarcher/Putnam, 1995), 133.

4

PREACHING TO THE SECULAR AGE

JOHN STARKE

Five years ago, I was sitting in a room full of pastors talking about the more challenging aspects of ministering in New York City. Our neighborhoods are diverse, so the challenges and frustrations were as well. Sitting in the corner, quietly listening, was an evangelical pastor serving in Paris, France. Through his broken English he said the challenges he was facing were not necessarily intolerance or intimidation, though that may be true in some cases. The biggest problem was that most people just didn't seem to care. Faith and God had little consequence. His neighbors did not see the need. Marginalization wasn't from persecution so much as apathy.

I came to realize that what we as pastors in our city were feeling may not primarily be hostility, but indifference. Our neighbors were simply happy living for goals and pleasures that take no account of God or transcendence.

I don't know if that was what everyone else in the room was thinking. Personally, this reason rang true because I happened to be reading Taylor's *A Secular Age* at the time. Taylor has long influenced religious philosophers and sociologists, but five years earlier *A Secular Age* had begun to shape the way ministers made sense of the communities we were serving. The dense and thick text made it difficult for many pastors to engage with the material, and since then resources and books have been written to help ministers and laypeople engage with its ideas. But I believe *A Secular Age* is a text worth the time, energy, and patience it will demands.

Amid everything else the book attempts to accomplish, at its base, it helps the spiritual leader see that our modern society has come to embrace "self-sufficient humanism." According to Taylor, "I mean by this a humanism accepting *no final goals* beyond human flourishing, nor any allegiance to anything else beyond this flourishing. Of no previous society was this true."[58]

In other words, our neighbors don't find meaning and significance in anything beyond the immanent sphere—beyond success, sex, power, and relationships. Yet, at the same time, there is a "malaise" amid this self-sufficient humanism: "The sense can easily arise that we are missing something, cut off from something, that we are living behind a screen. . . . I am thinking much more of a wide sense of malaise at the disenchanted world, a sense of it as flat, empty, a multiform search for something within, or beyond it, which could compensate for the meaning lost with transcendence."[59]

There is a fear and anxiety that "our actions, goals, achievements, and life, have a lack of weight, gravity, thickness, substance. There is a deeper resonance which they lack, which we feel should be there."[60] There is, then, a temptation among the secular toward transcendence. We cannot seem to live without it.

---

58   Taylor, *A Secular Age*, 18.
59   Ibid., 302.
60   Ibid., 307.

At the same time, we Christians live and breathe in this secular age as well. This self-sufficient humanism becomes part of the muscle memory of our own souls, even if we are often unconscious to its effect. What Taylor tells us about secularists hits awfully close to home in the pews. So, then, while modern self-sufficient secularists are tempted toward belief, believers are constantly tempted toward self-sufficiency.

The task of the preacher, it seems, is to aim at this dual temptation. We speak to the longings of those outside the faith and the wanderings of those inside. Taylor is a guide of sorts for pastors, providing an imprecise description of how our hearts have been formed as a society. I don't say "imprecise" in critique; I'm simply observing that what he says about society in general, pastors will have to explore in particular through personal stories and histories.

Within Taylor's 800 pages can be found helpful narratives and categories that provide deeper insight into our cultural moment. We have become a disenchanted age, and Taylor shows us why and how.

I want to narrow down three basic elements of Taylor's project that will seem more immediate for pastors and preachers in their work: (1) The Buffered Self, (2) The Malaise of Modernity, and (3) The Age of Authenticity.

THE BUFFERED SELF

The basic difference between a buffered self of the modern age and a porous self of earlier eras is the question of vulnerability. In previous centuries, it was assumed that we were vulnerable to spirits, both evil and good, and could be affected by the "presence" of something beyond the human and physical.[61] For example, not only did Martin Luther throw ink wells at the Devil while he translating the New Testament in the 16th century, he also ministered to communities who believed the forest was enchanted with ghosts and goblins. Ancients and pre-moderns believed in an enchanted world and saw themselves as vulnerable and porous selves. The powers could be malevolent or benevolent, pagan or Christian. A porous self sees not only that he is vulnerable to danger from these powers; a porous self also gains meaning and significance from outside himself.

But this sense of vulnerability has disappeared with the buffered self. "Things beyond don't need to 'get to me.'"[62] A buffered self "sees itself as invulnerable, as master of the meaning of things for it."[63] That last sentence is important: The self becomes the "master of the meaning of things." In other words, belief in God has not completely disappeared; we simply no longer need him for meaning and significance. A buffered self "blocks out certain ways in which transcendence has historically impinged on humans, and been present in their lives."[64] To put it more directly, here we have what Robert Bellah calls "expressive individualism."[65] This form of individualism sees its highest devotion to personal human flourishing. If one is to believe in God or a god, it must primarily be in service to human flourishing. The modern per-

---

61   For Taylor's explanation of the "buffered self" see Chapter 1, "The Bulwarks of Belief."

62   Ibid., 38.

63   Ibid.

64   Ibid., 239.

65   See Robert N. Bellah, Richard Madsen, William M. Sullivan, Ann Swidler, Steven M. Tipton, *Habits of the Heart: Individualism and Commitment in American Life* (Berkeley, CA: University of California Press, 1985).

son, a buffered self, who sees personal human flourishing as his or her highest commitment then sees every relationship or obligation (personal, relational, religious, or communal) as merely and only as an enhancement to the primary commitment to personal flourishing. "Thus, by a variety of routes, one could end up rejecting Christianity, because in calling for something more than human flourishing, it was the implacable enemy of the human good; and at the same time a denial of the dignity of the self-sufficient buffered identity."[66]

Christianity is not a means to human flourishing. In fact, Christianity instructs us to die to self, consider others more important, turn the cheek, offer ourselves as a living sacrifice, enter into weeping and sadness with others. This, of course, creates a conflict with the modern buffered self. The buffered self sees God and neighbor as enhancements that we can take or leave when they become burdensome or demand sacrifice. Christianity sees them as obligations rather than enhancements. Meaning, morality, and satisfaction come from without the self in Christianity. A buffered self seeks all that from within.

Pastors and other church leaders must recognize that their neighbors have internalized this way of thinking and often view any religious commitments as intruding on their self-sufficiency. But we must also see that our churches are potentially filled with people who see their current church commitments and investments into community as enhancements to their flourishing. When these "enhancements" begin to impede our "flourishing" by asking for sacrifice and demanding discomfort, the temptation will be to put off faith as an intolerable intruder to their buffered self. This may not be a conscious or explicitly stated condition. But it is the way

66   Taylor, *A Secular Age*, 264.

hearts are formed in the West today, whether or not someone is religious.

THE MALAISE OF MODERNITY

A buffered self offers many benefits. It provides a sense of freedom from the traditional mores of authoritarian societies and the "unenlightened masses," a "sense of power, of capacity, in being able to order our world and ourselves," a sense of invulnerability that takes away a fear of a world of spirits and forces, a "sense of self-possession, [and] a secure inner mental realm."[67] However, with that freedom comes a sense of "missing something, [being] cut off from something, [like] that we are living behind a screen."[68] It is what Taylor calls a sense of "malaise," which senses the world to be a flat, empty place, where what we've gained with our buffered selves doesn't compensate for what we've lost with transcendence.

The malaise deepens because even though we have given up on transcendent reality, we haven't given up on transcendent feelings and experiences. We instead look for transcendence within an imminent frame, which only exposes the smallness of our reality and intensifies the sense of loss. Taylor describes the malaise in three forms.[69]

First, we struggle to find significance in life. How do we gain a "higher goal" that transcends and gives meaning to all the lower ones? You could say, without a *telos* from some transcendent place outside ourselves, our lives have a fragility of meaning. Is my life going somewhere? A minister will

---

67   Taylor lays out the positive side of a buffered self in Taylor, *A Secular Age*, 300–01.

68   Ibid., 302.

69   See ibid., 308–09.

need to consistently point to the fragility of meaning outside of transcendence.

Second, crucial moments in life such as birth, marriage, and death heighten the sense of malaise. Traditionally, we have solemnized these moments by connecting them to something transcendent. "But an enclosure in the immanent leaves a hole here. Many people who have no other connection or felt affinity with religion, go on using the ritual of the church for these rites de passage."[70]

Third, we perceive a lack in everyday moments, in the mundane. "[S]ome people sense a terrible flatness in the everyday, and this experience has been identified particularly with commercial, industrial, or consumer society."[71] There is an "emptiness to the repeated, accelerating cycle of desire and fulfillment in consumer culture."[72] We, as buffered selves, sense a malaise, but because we seek solutions from within the immanent frame, our solutions do not work.

Pastors and other spiritual leaders must recognize and show their congregations the unsatisfying end of the buffered self, which sees human flourishing as its ultimate commitment and all other commitment (communal or religious) as mere enhancements that can be discarded when they no longer enhance. The buffered self ultimately alienates us from meaning, satisfaction, intimacy, and love.

A buffered self has been freed from transcendence and all its moral and religious obligations, but it has also been emptied of fullness along the way, leaving only a nagging sadness. The pastoral work for ministers is to tempt the secularist with fullness and joy to follow Christ, who had joy set

---

70   Taylor, *A Secular Age*, 309.
71   Ibid.
72   Ibid.

before him, even while he set aside human flourishing as he endured the cross (Heb. 12:2). Christians have known all along that human flourishing (or fullness) comes indirectly. Christianity teaches that if you die to yourself and participate with Christ in faith and obedience, you get human flourishing in the form of joy, a fruit of the Spirit. But if you aim at human flourishing, you will only get malaise.

AGE OF AUTHENTICITY

"Let's call this the Age of Authenticity," Taylor says.[73] We're committed to personal human flourishing, and we find that flourishing within ourselves. So our spirituality must be driven by "authentic" emotions that come from within, never from mere obedience or "theological correctness."[74] Our sexuality, likewise, is faithful primarily to internal desires, not to cultural or moral expectations. To put it differently, our modern secular culture disciples our hearts to be true to ourselves, to reject all outside intrusions.

There is a form of authenticity that attracts Christians and churchgoers without reference to Christian ethics. This authenticity boasts of the "weakness" or "messiness" of life. Leaders can gain a following by showing the "raw" elements of their life, the imperfections, the "beauty of the chaos." But this too is often a form of the buffered self. These confessions

---

73   Taylor, *A Secular Age*, 476.

74   Taylor (*A Secular* Age, 448) suggests: "This was the case, for instance, with Pietism and Methodism, for whom a powerful emotional response to God's saving action was more important than theological correctness." As with most of Taylor's comments concerning the Reformation and other Protestant movements, qualifications need to be kept in mind.

of imperfection come on our own terms. It is a *laissez-faire* spirituality that boasts of weakness but is buffered from criticism and reproof. Christianity is quite different. Christianity, too, boasts of weakness (see the apostle Paul), but makes the self vulnerable (different from merely authentic) to change and transformation.

The authentic self says, "This is me; you must accept me as I am." The vulnerable self says, "This is me; take me and transform me." The vulnerable self comes in the form not merely of confession but of repentance. It looks not to self for power and affirmation, but to divine help and deliverance.

None of these three elements will necessarily surprise the Christian minister. The Bible shows that these issues are more ancient than uniquely modern. Yet Taylor shows us how they manifest themselves today and how we might aim the truth of Christ with more precision. The Bible already warns us the self is impoverished apart from the riches of Christ. Taylor, however, shows us how individuals in Western society are feeling the impoverishment, even though they may not articulate it that way. He gives the pastor or church leader tools to tempt buffered selves with fullness of joy.

5

MILLENNIAL BELIEF IN THE SUPER-NOVA

DEREK RISHMAWY

I first read most of Taylor's *A Secular Age* one summer during my 5 a.m. shift at the gym. At the time, the main draw was Taylor's sprawling genealogy of Western secularism. The story of moving from an age where faith in God is the default to the point where it is an option was (and is) a fascinating tour through intellectual history.

As a Protestant, I later came to take Taylor's (Roman Catholic) historical tour with a grain of salt. But I realized the true value of Taylor's analysis while working in college and young adult ministry. His skill and insight as a contemporary tour guide—his ability to give you the lay of the sociological landscape—is invaluable.[75]

---

75   James K. A. Smith (*How [Not] to Be Secular*, 3) calls it a topographic relief map, giving us a feel for the age: "At its heart, *A Secular Age* is charting terrain mapped by the likes of Camus and Death Cab for Cutie more than staid social scientists and philosophers."

In this brief engagement with Taylor's work, I want to focus on a few threads surrounding the conditions of belief in order to see what light they shed on the challenges and opportunities involved in reaching that most-maligned and over-analyzed of generations: my fellow millennials.

BELIEF IN THE AGE OF THE SUPER-NOVA

Most analysis of millennials likes to focus on what makes them distinct. But a key point to keep in mind is that, in many respects, they're just like everyone else—but more so. In other words, they reflect major trends of the last couple of generations, simply a bit farther down the line of historical and logical progression. Like everybody else, they live in the epistemological and moral atmosphere Taylor dubs the "Nova Effect."[76]

As Taylor explains, 500 years ago belief in God was the default; fulfilled, humane atheism was akin to belief in unicorns today. With "modernity" and the Enlightenment came the rise of "exclusive humanism" (humanistic atheism) as a viable alternative to Christian faith. The ensuing explosion of polemics between skeptics, Deists, believers, and Romantics triggered a chain reaction resulting in a constantly multiplying diversity of spiritual options. The Nova Effect has become "a kind of galloping pluralism on the spiritual plane."[77]

Practically, this Nova Effect means several things. First, we're all cross-pressured by dozens of options, leaving everybody's beliefs "fragilized" and destabilized. If you're a theist, you still feel the draw of immanence—as you sit in your room, watching the latest Netflix documentary about the cosmos,

---

76   Taylor, *A Secular Age*, 299–321.
77   Ibid., 300.

belief in a godless universe is *imaginable* at an intellectual and existential level. But if you're a skeptic, transcendence beckons. Every hike you take on the local trail, God keeps haunting you with blades of sunlight filtering through the trees.

Put another way, we all know sane, rational people, living much the same as we do yet believing radically different things. Your Sikh neighbors, your Buddhist gym buddy, and your atheist co-worker buy groceries at the same niche food shop, catch the Marvel franchise of superhero flicks, and love their families. But none of them goes to your church on Sunday.[78] There are no more singular, monolithic, obvious takes on the world. Belief has become less of an on/off switch, and more of a series of dials you can set in various degrees (post-secular, humanist, Romantic, libertarian, eco-feminist, and on and on).

So how do we set the dials today? In the Age of Authenticity (think life post-1960s), the drive is to make sure—whatever else may affect our decision—that we are "true to ourselves." This is how "expressive individualism" plays a role in belief formation.[79] Some of us may still choose traditional faiths like Roman Catholicism, evangelical Protestantism, or one of the other major world religions. But nobody simply *inherits* packages of beliefs anymore; we *choose* to believe (and

---

78   For a complementary account of how 20th-century U.S. immigration patterns played a role in fueling the Nova effect at the popular level, see David Wells, *Above All Earthly Pow'rs: Christ in a Postmodern World*, (Grand Rapids, MI: Eerdmans, 2005), 91–124.

79   For the original work on "expressive individualism," see Robert N. Bellah, Richard Madsen, William M. Sullivan, Ann Swidler, Steven M. Tipton, *Habits of the Heart*. One quote seems helpful (47): "Its genius is that it enables an individual to think of his commitments—from marriage to work to social

even construct) the packages for ourselves, often as part of our self-actualization project.

The resulting blends vary. One has a little bit of Christianity here, some therapeutic psychology there, and a dash of social justice progressivism to top it off. Another may choose a Buddhist base, some Western rationalism, and a commitment to exercise. The root of this "heretical imperative"[80] is a sense that spiritual beliefs aid the quest of finding our unique way of being human. We have become a nation of heretics,[81] or rather, syncretists.

SUPER-NOVA ON GOOGLE

Turning to what distinguishes millennials, it is important to note they vary even from one another. Still, one of the most significant markers distinguishing millennials from other generations is having grown up in the Internet Age. "Googling" as a verb was recognized by *Merriam-Webster's Dictionary* only 10 years ago, which means it has been in use even longer. For millennials that's anywhere between a third to half of our lifetime.

If we already lived in a religious Super-nova, the internet has only metastasized the problem. Skimming your

---

and religious involvement—as enhancements of the sense of individual well-being rather than as moral imperatives."

80 Peter Berger, *The Heretical Imperative: Contemporary Possibilities of Religious Affirmation* (New York, NY: Anchor Press, 1979).

81 See Ross Douthat's incisive jeremiad, *Bad Religion: How We Became a Nation of Heretics* (New York, NY: Free Press, 2012), especially the chapter "God Within" (211–41). Though focused on the sort of Oprahfied spirituality of Boomers, much of the analysis still applies to their "spiritual but not religious" millennial children.

Facebook newsfeeds, you're constantly bombarded by multiplying perspectives on politics, race, gender, and spirituality.[82] Never mind if you're curious and actually *looking* for different options.

A few things follow from this effect. First, Christianity has lost (a significant amount of) its home-court advantage. It is now one of a wide array of competitors on the market, some of which have the benefit of being significantly more malleable to the sexual and economic ethics of the late-modern West. Though Christianity still claims the highest market share of American millennials, this generation identifies as religiously unaffiliated at higher rates than any other generation (34 percent religious unaffiliated, 46 percent Christian).[83] That's not to say they're atheists, but they're not as prone to claim a specific religious tradition.

Second, the nature of authority in religion has shifted. Modernity has always had an inherently anti-authoritarian, anti-institutional, anti-clerical ethos. But the internet enables an even more radically individualistic and practical epistemology. Communities struggle in their traditional role as protective, authoritative sources of religious truth.

For example, being a religious professional means a lot less than it used to. Millennials don't feel the need to wait

---

82   On the role of the internet in encouraging the increasing fracturing of American culture into micro-cultures, both political and religious, see Yuval Levin, *Fractured Republic: Renewing America's Social Contract in the Age of Individualism* (New York, NY: Basic Books, 2016), especially the discussion in chapter 6, "The Subculture Wars" (147–84).

83   Michael Lipka, "Millennials Increasingly are driving growth of nones," *Pew Research Center* (May 12, 2015). http://www.pewresearch.org/fact-tank/2015/05/12/ millennials-increasingly-are-driving-growth-of-nones/

for a pastor to tell them the best reading of a verse. What does a seminary degree count for when you can just Google anything yourself?[84] What's more, if you don't like what your pastor says, you can look up alternatives in the middle of the sermon on your phone—which you probably know how to use better than he does. Indeed, millennials' greater aptitude for technology has also helped shift the locus of authority from age to youth—kids teach their grandparents to use gear they navigate as second-nature.[85] The older need the younger more than the younger believe they need the older. And they don't see any irony about publishing memoirs in their 20s.

HEROIC DOUBT AND THE POST-EVANGELICAL APPEAL

Not unlike previous generations, the millennial maturation story sets them against their elders. One of Taylor's most important apologetic moves explains how conversion to atheism or exclusive humanism is motivated by a particular moral narrative. It isn't simply a matter of being faced with "the science," following a syllogism to its logical conclusion, and deciding God doesn't add up. Instead, deconversion is more of a decision to follow a particular story about belief and doubt.

In this story, doubt is the movement of a heroic individual stepping into intellectual adulthood and maturity, no

---

84   Indeed, this isn't only a matter of millennials and religious authority. "Expertise" is on life-support across disciplines and generations. See Tom Nichols, *The Death of Expertise: The Campaign Against Established Knowledge and Why it Matters* (New York, NY: Oxford University Press, 2017).

85   See Carl Trueman, *The Creedal Imperative* (Wheaton, IL: Crossway, 2012), 26–27, for his apt comments on the way "the flow of knowledge has been reversed" from the old to the young.

matter the cost. Moving to an exclusive humanism away from their earlier, childish faith requires virtues "such as disengaged reason, the courage to let go of comforting illusions, the reliance on one's own reason against authority."[86] Though not easy, doubt is brave, strong, and daring.[87]

Consider, then, the recent wave of post-evangelical memoirs centered on the spiritual journeys of young writers—and their appeal for millennials. While diverse, such memoirs tend to bear some commonalities. These first-person narratives of faith-discovery as self-discovery do not resemble the typical faith-hero stories of the past. Rather, they tend to valorize doubt and uncertainty.[88] And this fits with the broader cultural scripts of broken faith on offer in present media culture.[89]

---

86   Taylor, *A Secular Age*, 566.

87   Recall Immanuel Kant's famous opening paragraph to his programmatic essay "An Answer to the Question: What is Enlightenment?": "Enlightenment is man's emergence from his self-imposed immaturity. Immaturity is the inability to use one's own understanding without the guidance of another. This immaturity is self-imposed if its cause lies not in lack of understanding but in indecision and lack of courage to use one's own mind without another's guidance. The motto of enlightenment is therefore: *Sapere aude!* Have the courage to use your own understanding!" in *Kant's Political Writings*, 2nd. ed., trans. H. B. Nisbet, Ed. H. S. Reiss, (New York, NY: Cambridge University Press, 1991), 54.

88   For a helpful analysis of this genre and typical works, see Alastair Roberts's brief eBook, *The New Storytellers*. https://alastairadversaria.files.wordpress.com/2016/10/the-new-storytellers2.pdf

89   Kevin Vanhoozer ("What Is Everyday Theology? How and Why Christians Should Read Culture," in *Everyday Theology: How to Read Cultural Texts and Interpret Trends*, ed. Kevin J.

The particular struggles and doubts differ from title to title. Some wrestle with issues of belief, anti-intellectualism, and science in search of something better than pat answers to hard questions. Others flee the legalistic, exhausting, abusive spirituality of their fundamentalist and evangelical communities. Still more focus on the challenge of reconsidering church stances on sex and/or gay marriage.[90]

Whatever the issue, though, the existential and cognitive dissonance in the face of these cross-pressured and fragilizing conditions becomes too much for their former faith. The protagonists emerge into a new phase of faith—maybe broken and bruised, a bit uncertain, but more authentic, risky, and in possession of a faith truly their own. Baptized in the fires of doubt, they have left behind the simpler, naive

---

Vanhoozer, Charles A. Anderson, Michael J. Sleasman [Grand Rapids, MI: Baker, 2007], 29): "Whereas past cultural texts showed us how to live a life of faith, the texts of today's popular culture enact scripts of broken faith: of defiance or anger toward God; of fear of an indifferent or oppressive reality; of escape from sorrow over the absent God by finding joy in one's immediate mundane life."

90   If you're looking for a good representative, consult the various works of Rachel Held Evans, whose theological and personal progression is both archetypal and also influential. See *Faith Unraveled: How a Girl Who Knew All the Answers Learned to Ask Questions* (Grand Rapids, MI: Zondervan, 2014); idem., *A Year of Biblical Womanhood: How a Liberated Woman Found Herself Sitting on Her Roof, Covering Her Head, and Calling Her Husband "Master"* (Nashville, TN: Thomas Nelson, 2012); idem., *Searching for Sunday: Loving, Leaving, and Finding the Church* (Nashville, TN: Thomas Nelson, 2015). On this last, see my review at The Gospel Coalition (https://www.thegospelcoalition.org/article/searching-for-sunday).

beliefs of their shallow, therapeutic youth group (and their parents). They have dared to know.

My point isn't so much to critique these stories—some raise valid critiques that ought to be heard—but simply to note their connection to the ethics of belief under the Nova Effect. The ethic of heroic-doubt-as-maturity explains at least some of their appeal. Some memoir writers are quick to admit they're offering one "take" on the world, with the apparent humility to know it is not the only plausible one on offer.[91] Others relieve the tension by simply restructuring beliefs to fit the different pressures (even if that involves rewriting 2,000 years of received teaching). More importantly, though, they recognize the need for breathing space as ordinary believers feel disoriented, undecided, full of questions, and burned out.

Thus these narratives generate an alternative form of spiritual and moral authority—the authority of authenticity. In the Age of Authenticity, a testimony of suffering, struggle, and doubt earns you the right to be heard. And not only heard, but even followed as a model—not of infallible truth, but of an empathetic, authentic, fellow doubter who won't be quick to pass judgment on our weaknesses; one who reveals to us the strength we can find in the midst of those weaknesses.

---

91   Taylor talks about two ways of inhabiting the cross-pressured space we all share in the immanent frame (*A Secular Age*, 549–551). On Taylor's view, everybody has a deep sense of the way things are, a "take" on the world, whether open or closed to transcendence. To adopt your take as "spin" is to take an overconfident stance about the world, convincing yourself your take is really just "obvious" and clear, unwilling to admit the plausibility of other stances.

MINISTRY IN THE SUPER-NOVA

With these factors in mind, how then, shall we minister to millennials in the Super-nova?

Shun Despair and Nostalgia

First, we need to refuse the temptation to despair, or to engage in a morose, crippling nostalgia for some mythical, lost Golden Age of Faith. As Taylor points out, earlier ages may not have suffered from the struggles of pluralism, fragilization, and cross-pressures. But surely in Christendom there was a greater temptation to spiritual authoritarianism, hypocrisy, and the shallow "belief" of social conformity.

Indeed, Kierkegaard wrote a dozen books under half as many pseudonyms trying to explain to Christendom that New Testament Christianity wasn't simply a matter of "having a baptismal certificate lying in the drawer and producing it when one is to be a student or wants to have a wedding."[92] Fed up and unheard, at the end of his life he launched his blistering, all-out "attack on Christendom" that should give us all pause before waxing too nostalgic for a ministry in the cultural Christianity of yesteryear.[93] If our context presses us to preach a sincere faith to our millennial hearers, why not receive this as a charge from the Lord?

---

92   Søren Kierkegaard, *Concluding Unscientific Postscript to Philosophical Fragments*, vol. 1, trans. Howard V. Hong and Edna Hong, Kierkegaard's Writings, XII.1 (Princeton, NJ: Princeton University Press, 1992), 367.

93   See Søren Kierkegaard, *Attack Upon "Christendom,"* trans. Walter Lowrie (Princeton, NJ: Princeton University Press, 1944).

Preach Apologetically

We must also maximize what advantages this age affords us. Materialism and exclusive humanism don't have the automatic upper hand in the Age of Authenticity. While in earlier decades Christianity may have been considered the default religion in the West, materialism and atheism held sway in elite circles as the more obviously intellectual option. But since the Super-nova doesn't translate into atheism outright, more intellectual breathing room has been created for "spiritual" conversation. Christians still have an opportunity to present the gospel as a beautiful alternative to the cramped ideologies of immanence that dominate our landscape.

We've reached the point where everybody has to preach apologetically, even if your congregation isn't mostly millennial. To be clear, I don't think such preaching is simply a matter of incorporating in every sermon arguments for the resurrection, or the existence of God, and so forth (though some of that might help). Instead, we need to actively answer objections to the gospel from *inside* the mindset of our cross-pressured culture on a regular basis as a part of our scriptural exposition. We need to show the consistency, coherence, and comeliness of the gospel to this generation.

But it is not enough to simply defend the gospel. Present the way it interrogates the dominant, unquestioned narratives of our hearers—on meaning, money, sex, power, politics, gender, and so forth—and actually makes better sense of the world than any other view on offer.

Taylor's *A Secular Age* is something of a model here, since the entire work destabilizes the stories secularists tell themselves about how they came by their unbelief. He doesn't so much "prove them wrong" as level the playing the field, poking holes in their accounts.[94] If you're curious what this looks like, read Tim Keller.[95]

There are at least a couple of payoffs when we preach apologetically. First, we make clear that the gospel claims to be truth. That focus helps keep Christianity from being adopted as just another self-expressive spirituality, chosen because "it works for me." Second, it begins to address the actual questions and struggles of many millennials. Even if we can't answer every question, we can begin to show them there is a robust, intellectual tradition of Christian reflection on these issues beyond the half-remembered lessons they received in Sunday school. The right kind of apologetic preaching acknowledges pressure on belief even as it works to present Christianity from within that pressurized environment.

Make Space for Thomas

Here I think of the story of Thomas—our quintessential doubter. When he heard the other disciples' testimony, he did not believe (John 20:25). He had not seen the risen Christ, and refused to believe until he did. A couple of points stand out for our purposes.

For the next week, Thomas remained with them—an unbeliever in the midst of disciples filled with resurrection hope (John 20:26). It is as if they knew the scandalous absur-

---

94   James K. A. Smith (*How (Not) to Be Secular*, 120–21) calls attention to its similarity to the moves of Reformed Epistemologists like Alvin Plantinga and Nicholas Wolterstorff.

95   I'm not joking. All of his directly apologetic works are relevant here, since he explicitly puts Taylor to use. But see especially Timothy Keller, *Preaching: Communicating Faith in an Age of Skepticism* (New York, NY: Viking, 2015). And don't skip the endnotes.

dity of what had be revealed to them, so they patiently made space for him until the Lord visited.

Likewise churches interested in reaching millennials need to become skilled in that sort of patience that graciously makes space for the questioner, the cross-pressured unbeliever. The church must not be a place prone to overreaction, or quick to provide conversation-stopping clichés (which inadvertently produce reactive questioners). Questions and dialogue must be welcome.[96]

This approach actually calls for a more robust ecclesiology and community, rather than a thin one. Churches with strong practices of membership and discipline actually have the stability required to include someone without destabilizing the community or undermining its confession.[97]

Making space for Thomas also requires a certain amount of humble confidence that trusts in the Lord to eventually vindicate our faith. Non-defensive assurance in the truth of the gospel attracts many younger millennials. Not everybody needs to go through a faith crisis to earn the requisite amount of authenticity points to minister to millennials. While we "cannot imagine that any certainty that is not tinged with

---

96   On the importance of creating "communities of inquiry," see Matthew Lee Anderson, *The End of Our Exploring: A Book About Questioning and the Confidence of Faith* (Chicago, IL: Moody, 2013), 125–142.

97   Incidentally, this is also the sort of community that will prioritize things like properly catechizing its own children in the present. Many of the failures of the evangelical church over the last 20 years with respect to millennials can be connected to the therapeutic assumptions of its youth groups (which only matched that of the main pulpits), and thin practices of discipleship and worship.

doubt,"[98] we shouldn't concede that someone is "particular-ly truthful, deep, fine, and elegant because of his doubt."[99] Indeed, we may leverage the Age of Authenticity to our advantage by pushing back on the notion that authentic faith *requires* a crisis. Making space for Thomas shouldn't require becoming just like him.

More than the disciples, Jesus himself is our model for dealing with Thomas. He comes to him, graciously accepting him, unworried and unperturbed by his questions. He meets Thomas on his own terms in order to invite him to faith—"A bruised reed he shall not break" (Isa. 42:3).

Ultimately, though, churches must depend on Jesus's words to Thomas: "Because you have seen me, you have believed; blessed are those who have not seen and yet have believed" (John 20:29). There is blessing for those who walk by faith and not by sight. Jesus has prayed for them, and the Father has heard him (John 17:20). This promise is for us and for the cross-pressured millennials we seek to serve for the sake of the gospel. Christ has gone to the cross for them, and he will not lose any of them given to him by his Father—not even in a Secular Age.

---

98   John Calvin, *Institutes of the Christian Religion,* ed. John T. Mc-Neill, trans. Ford Lewis Battles (Philadelphia, PA: Westmin-ster, 1960), III.2.17, 562.

99   Karl Barth, *Evangelical Theology: An Introduction* (Grand Rapids, MI: Eerdmans, 1963), 132.

6

LITURGICAL PIETY

ALASTAIR ROBERTS

In his exploration of the liturgy of the fourth and fifth centuries in *Introduction to Liturgical Theology*, Alexander Schmemann discusses the phenomena of "liturgical piety."[100] While many historians of the liturgy have focused exclusively on the objective and formal dimensions of the liturgy, Schmemann directs our attention to the shifting "religious sense" that has been brought to it. Even when the objective forms of the liturgy have remained constant, changes in the religious sense people have brought to the liturgy can mark dramatic transformations in the experience and perception of Christian worship. Where changes in liturgies occur, such shifts in the religious sense of an age of worshipers will often be the cause.

> Above all it is important for the historian of worship
> to know that the "liturgical piety" of an epoch can in
> various ways fail to correspond to the liturgy or cult
> of which this piety is nevertheless the psychological

---

100   Alexander Schmemann, *Introduction to Liturgical Theology*, trans. Asheleigh E. Moorehouse (Crestwood, NY: St. Vladimir's Seminary Press, 2003), 97–98.

perception or experience. This means that piety can
accept the cult in a "key" other than that in which it
was conceived and expressed as text, ceremony or "rite."
Liturgical piety has the strange power of "transposing"
texts or ceremonies, of attaching a meaning to them
which is not their plain or original meaning.[101]

Schmemann argues that such a shift in religious sense
occurred as Christianity rose to prominence after Constan-
tine. He reminds readers that paganism was far more than
mere idols that could be destroyed and temples that could
be demolished:

> [P]aganism, which the Church had been fighting with
> all of her strength, was not so much a doctrine as it was
> a cosmic feeling in the deepest organic way with the
> whole fabric of the social, political and economic life of
> the times.[102]

Although the church's worship may have remained much the
same in its objective form, as the church filled the place in
the social imaginary that paganism had vacated, the meaning
of its liturgical practice became severely distorted as it was
refracted through the "mysteriological" piety of paganism.

The effect of this mysteriological piety was to cast the
liturgy as a sanctifying cult, akin to the mystery cults' mode
of religion. The mystery religions offered saving cults with
the dramatically re-enacted myths that served them, whereas
Christianity presented a saving faith that answered to the

---

101   Schmemann, *Introduction to Liturgical Theology*, 97.
102   Ibid., 112.

once-for-all work of Christ in history.[103] The mystery cults served as means of "sanctification," separating the sacred and the profane, conferring sacred status through ceremonies and rituals, whereas Christian liturgy was the faithful action of the church, by which its eschatological character in Christ was manifested.

Under the influence of mysteriological piety, Christian worship was subtly yet markedly transformed. Clergy and cult, by which the desired sanctification was effected, began to eclipse the congregation and liturgy as the "work of the people." Buildings came to be regard as sacred and sanctifying, and cults began to develop around particular holy sites.[104] As they were perceived and approached differently, ceremonies became increasingly elaborate and grand, embellished with the accretions of many attendant rites, all designed to produce a more awe-inspiring liturgical drama to answer the desire for sanctifying rite.

SECULARISM'S SOCIAL IMAGINATION AND CHRISTIAN LITURGY

At the heart of Taylor's work in *A Secular Age* is the question of the "whole context of understanding in which our moral, spiritual or religious experience and search takes place."[105] Although Taylor foregrounds the conditions and framing of unbelief, the cultural shifts he identifies are also critically important for understanding contemporary forms of Christian faith and practice. If the social imaginary of paganism framed much of the Constantinian reception and development of the

---

103 Schmemann, *Introduction to Liturgical Theology*, 107–08.
104 Ibid., 113–18.
105 Taylor, *A Secular Age*, 3.

liturgy, the secularism Taylor's work explores plays a corresponding role in our own social environment.

Without rehearsing the lineaments of Taylor's broader thesis here, I want to highlight a few dimensions of his account of secularism that bear on our practice of liturgy.

First, the "buffered self" Taylor identifies as the modern form of the subject has a clear boundary or "buffer" between the internal self and the external world. Meaning that would once have been embedded in the external world and the community now withdraws into the individual self. With the loss of an "enchanted world," the buffered self becomes the master of its own meanings, and the possibility of disengagement becomes more real. In contrast to such a being, the "porous self" is open and vulnerable to the natural and social world it inhabits, in which it encounters meaning.

As meaning is relocated from the external and social world into the private and buffered world of the individual mind, our experience of Christian liturgy shifts, and the locus of its meaning is dispersed. Although we may continue to practice the liturgy as a common and collective rite, like a large pond that has steadily drained out through hundreds of plug holes, its meaning now increasingly resides in the privacy of worshipers' minds, rather than in the shared space and action that unites us.

The modern buffered self struggles to comport itself in manner that makes possible robust communal participation in an objectively meaningful ritual that has the power to impose its meanings on us and which opens us to divine blessing or judgment. When we celebrate something such as the Eucharist as modern selves, we can perceive its meaning to occur in the privacy of our minds, rather than in the external socio-symbolic and objective realm we share. With this shift in the locus of meaning, key facets of the biblical teaching concerning the Supper—not least its character as *communion* with each other in the body of Christ—can be obscured.

Second, Taylor describes an "age of authenticity," characterized by "expressive individualism," within which each of us must forge for ourselves whatever bespoke form of identity rests most comfortably on our shoulders.[106] Central to this age of authenticity are spaces of "mutual display" within which many individuals exist in a "horizontal, simultaneous mutual presence."[107] These spaces "hover between solitude and togetherness," occasionally moving into the realm of common action (e.g. in the protest march) or common emotion (e.g. in the rock concert).[108] In these "lonely crowds," we each perform our own individuality in conformist or alienated ways. We identify with others, affiliate with particular groups, consume defining products, and adopt specific styles in ways that signal our own identities to those around us.

This age of authenticity is one in which consumption plays a crucial role: various companies provide us with the images, styles, and brands by which we can fashion our identities for ourselves and signal them to others. Taylor was writing at the outset of the revolutionary rise of online social media; ten years later, his observations have never seemed more pertinent. Social media like Facebook or Twitter are some of the purest examples of spaces of mutual display. In the world of online social media, cut loose from the heavily textured fabric of concrete society and its differentiated identities, we are all reduced to cookie-cutter individual profiles. We each choose our own affiliations, defining ourselves by patterns and objects of consumption and the image we

---

106   Smith, *How (Not) To Be Secular*, 85.
107   Taylor, *Secular Age*, 481.
108   Ibid., 482.

present of ourselves for others. The identities forged in such a manner are themselves commodified for the use of advertisers to sell us more products and services. The intensity of this shared realm of display can produce an acute self-reflexivity, akin to perceiving one's face in a mirror for the first time.

Within the age of authenticity, we can approach Christian liturgy chiefly as a means of self-expression, and forget its character as communal action and formation. While many speak of their desire for "community," the community they seek is often of an ersatz character, participating only in the shallow and fleeting "community" that can be enjoyed in the "lonely crowd." Churches can attempt to achieve "community" through affected informality and friendliness or through the elevated emotions of the music-driven worship event, which may produce a similar effect to the rock concert. We have identified community with a feeling that can be synthesized, rather than a bond of deep mutual commitment and the shared disciplines that powerfully and enduringly unite us in the pursuit and celebration of common objects of love. Mark Searle writes of such worship:

> We take part because we choose to do so, and we choose to do so because we like it, or it makes us feel good about ourselves, or because we enjoy praying and singing with others. It gives an evanescent experience of togetherness, a passing *frisson* of religious excitement, but it doesn't impose the constraints of discipline and commitment. It merely satisfies some obscurely felt need for the time being but will have to be fresh and different and exciting every time if it is to keep drawing us back.[109]

---

109   Anne Y. Koester and Barbara Searle, eds., *Vision: The Scholarly Contributions of Mark Searle to Liturgical Renewal* (Collegeville,

Even the return to traditional liturgy that one finds in some circles can be driven by the same underlying forces of expressive individualism. Rather than a submission to authority, tradition can be an attractive consumer choice for those in search of "authenticity" in a society where many options on offer seem to lack the weight and beauty of long-established custom. Attending a church with a higher liturgy can be a worshiper's means of signaling refinement, elevated aesthetic judgment, ecclesiastical pedigree, and socio-economic class. In such cases, tradition may be valued principally for its vintage feel or ancient dignity, rather than for the truth that first animated its creation.[110]

Third, Taylor speaks of the uprooting of music, poetry, and other human works of creation from the worlds and contexts to which they once belonged, and their reestablishment as autonomous "art."[111] What was once the elevation of social action to a higher register through beauty—such as in the "privileged way of speaking to God, or being in communion with him" that constitutes the liturgy—gradually became a non-participatory object of contemplation, and then a pure autonomous work of art.[112]

Art retains its power to move us. But as art is disembedded, first from communal action and then even from collective contemplation, this experience of being moved is detached from the proper object of the work of art. It can become a pure aesthetic experience, untethered from the

---

MN: Liturgical Press, 2004), 194.

110   Louis-Marie Chauvet, *Symbol and Sacrament: A Sacramental Reinterpretation of Christian Existence*, trans. Patrick Madigan and Madeleine Beaumont (Collegeville, MN: Liturgical Press, 1995), 332–33.

111   Smith, *How (Not) To Be Secular*, 74–75.

112   Taylor, *Secular Age*, 354.

object it was originally intended to serve. Such art still affords a sense of transcendence, but a "transcendence" cut loose from the objective transcendence to which it once related. As we become accustomed to perceiving art as autonomous, our perception of the liturgy can change. The liturgy can be approached as if an aesthetic spectacle, evoking feelings of transcendence in us, yet without a clear connection to its true object or a deep foundation in common action.

REFORMING LITURGICAL PIETY IN A SECULAR AGE

These three dimensions of Taylor's account of secularization are merely representative; several more such examples could be listed. Yet together they serve to illustrate that, even where traditional liturgies remain unchanged, the imagination with which it is encountered has changed markedly.

Through the work of writers such as James K. A. Smith (one of Taylor's appreciative interpreters), many evangelicals are thankfully discovering the liturgy's power to shape imagination and form a renewed *habitus* in those who practice it. Yet within this revival in evangelical liturgical appreciation has been a dearth of reflection on the fact that the movement between liturgy and imagination isn't unidirectional, and a failure to reckon adequately with the degree to which our liturgies can be radically transformed by the prevailing social imaginary. In Smith's insightful treatment of worship in *Imagining the Kingdom*, for instance, the need for liturgical catechesis and preaching to prevent the misappropriation of the liturgy is foregrounded only as a concluding afterthought, within a book that speaks much about the way that liturgy comports us to truth in a secular age.[113]

Writing in a Roman Catholic context, Searle observes a disproportionate emphasis placed on reforming the images of the liturgy to overcome the disconnect between the people and traditional Christian worship.[114] Yet the *imagination* with which modern worshipers encounter the liturgy had been neglected:

> [T]he imagination itself was never made the subject of conscious and critical reflection, and this may be part of the reason why, after all the changes that have occurred, the expected renewal of Church life has come to something of a stalemate. . . . The imagination is not what we see or think: it is rather the lens through which we see, the very patterns within which we think.[115]

The challenge that Christian liturgy faces in contemporary society is that the imaginations it encounters have undergone and are undergoing rigorous formation into ways of seeing and acting that are quite contrary to the world it projects. Even when the necessity of rehabituation is appreciated, we need to be able to ensure a minimal level of appropriate engagement with the liturgy to initiate this process. That the liturgy will, with sufficient repetition, bring the imagination around to an appropriate understanding is not self-evident. Would not evidence suggest that, with an imagination lacking the appropriate modes and postures of receptivity

---

113   James K. A. Smith, *Imagining the Kingdom: How Worship Works* (Grand Rapids, MI: Baker Academic, 2013), 186ff.
114   Koester and Searle, *Vision*, 128.
115   Ibid., 127.

to its images, the practice of the liturgy can fail to exert its intended transformative power—indeed that it might become a process of *malformation*? Repetition of etiolated liturgy may not be able to counteract the effect of a misguided liturgical piety by itself.

Here I believe evangelicals have much to learn from liturgical theologians such as Searle who, more than 30 years ago, spoke of the need for developing a third branch of liturgical studies, alongside historical research and the study of the theology of the liturgy.[116] Searle termed the new branch of liturgical studies he envisioned "pastoral liturgical studies." Gilbert Ostdiek describes its purpose:

> This new discipline will have three tasks. First, its *empirical task* is "to attend to what actually goes on in the rite" and to describe what is happening. Second, the *hermeneutical task* is to study "how symbols operate and how symbolic language communicates." Third, the *critical task* is to compare the previous two sets of findings "with the historical tradition and with the theological claims made for the liturgy" and to draw appropriate theological and pastoral conclusions.[117]

One of the central concerns of this discipline is to discover and address the areas of mismatch between the "imaginative world projected by the liturgy with the imaginative world out of which [contemporary persons] operate."[118] The gulf between these two worlds cannot be bridged from one side alone. Attending to wise analysts of contemporary secular

---

116   Koester and Searle, *Vision*, 101ff.
117   Ibid., 101.
118   Ibid., 115–16.

society such as Charles Taylor will be a necessary task for any who desire to reinvigorate liturgical practice in the current environment.

7

CHURCH SHOPPING WITH CHARLES TAYLOR

BRETT MCCRACKEN

There were many revolutions in North Atlantic civilization in the post-war era: a cultural revolution, a consumer revolution, a sexual revolution, an "individuating revolution,"[119] a revolution of youth culture, to name a few. It was a time of great tumult, in which various streams churned together in an explosive cauldron of profound change.

A major result of this volatile era, which Charles Taylor coins "The Age of Authenticity" in *A Secular Age*, has been the steady expansion of expressive individualism. Emerging from the Romantic expressivism of the late-18th century, this attitude of "authenticity" is that "each one of us has his/her own way of realizing our humanity, and that it's important to find and live out one's own, as against surrendering to conformity with a model imposed on us from outside, by society, or the previous generation, or religious or political authority."[120]

---

119   Taylor, *A Secular Age*, 473.
120   Ibid., 475.

This anti-institutional shift—which positioned the individual as the primary arbiter of authority and meaning—has wrought havoc on churches and religious institutions during the last several decades. In the social imaginary of expressive individualism, the sense that one's identity depends on "belonging to large-scale collective agencies"[121] like churches has been replaced by framing identity in consumerist terms: choice as an overarching value, celebrity and performance as ideals, individuated "style" as an existential necessity.

Autonomy and freedom are primary values in this Age of Authenticity. Autonomy leads to a soft relativism that proclaims, "[L]et each person do their own thing, and we shouldn't criticize each other's 'values.'"[122] Freedom pushes against any imposition or constraint or accountability—anything that questions one's decisions or intrudes on one's privacy.

This perspective fundamentally alters the role of faith in an individual's life. It becomes just another expression of identity that can be curated and enacted according to personal tastes and preferences and not according to any obligation or external expectation. In the Age of Authenticity, faith need not be encumbered by church and its rather distasteful impositions of authority/guidelines/accountability. This is a change. Not so long ago, spirituality was necessarily embedded within a church or religious institution. But in our present era, to be spiritual is simply to "accept what rings true to your own inner Self."[123]

---

121   Taylor, *A Secular Age*, 484.
122   Ibid.
123   Ibid., 489.

HOW DID WE GET HERE?

In *A Secular Age*, Taylor describes the gradual transition from
a "paleo-Durkheimian dispensation" where it was assumed
one's connection to the sacred entailed belonging to a
church, to a more consumer-friendly "neo-Durkheimian
dispensation," where it is possible for individuals to "enter the
denomination of my choice"—not by societal obligation but
simply because it "seems right."[124] This then gives way to a
non- or post-Durkheimian disposition, where expressive individualism leads churchgoers to talk about church in consumerist language of choice, preference, and comfort.

When churchgoing becomes mostly about finding the
church that best supports one's own subjective "spiritual
path," Taylor seems to suggest, it will eventually become
an impossible task, more frustrating and draining than it
is worth. As he notes, "If the focus is going now to be on
my spiritual path, thus on what insights come to me in the
subtler languages that I find meaningful, then maintaining
this or any other framework becomes increasingly difficult."[125]
Why? Because no church is ever going to be perfectly tailored
to my preferences and the "subtler languages" I find meaningful. Something will always make me bristle, something
will leave me feeling unseen, unheard, uncomfortable. Just
as we eventually grow tired of a trendy restaurant or favor-
ite clothing brand because our tastes inevitably change, so
we will eventually tire of a church that initially connects
with our unique "spiritual path" but then fails to sufficiently
track with our evolving beliefs. So we keep shopping for that

---

124   Taylor, *A Secular Age*, 486.
125   Ibid.

"perfect fit" church, or (more likely) we give up the futile search entirely.

Taylor's observations suggest that churches perpetuating the paradigm of church shopping are setting the stage for their own spiritual demise. By accepting the consumerist terms of the Age of Authenticity and seeing themselves as another product to be branded and marketed and consumed, churches merely amplify the instability. They encourage the fickle, commitment-phobic habits of consumers who attend only insofar as it fits the nuances of their personally curated spirituality.

But is there really any other option? Are churches in a secular age in any position to challenge or ignore the picky preferences and high standards of consumer churchgoers? Or must they come to terms with the church-shopping reality of the post-Durkheimian disposition, where religion—like any product or piece of media "content"—must compete for the attention of individuals in a crowded marketplace, just one among many options but by no means obligatory?

IS CHURCH SHOPPING THE NEW NORMAL?

Though he notes exceptions to the post-Durkheimian dispensation, Taylor seems to think we ought to come to terms with this trend as the new normal. There is now "no necessary embedding of our link to the sacred in any particular framework,"[126] no necessary accountability to some externally defined orthodoxy. "For many people today," he argues, "to set aside their own path in order to conform to some external authority just doesn't seem comprehensible as a form of

---

126   Taylor, *A Secular Age*, 487.

spiritual life."[127] The preferred mode of spirituality—framed as a personal quest—is allergic to "authority claims made by churches which see it as their mandate to preempt the search, or to maintain it within certain definite limits, and above all to dictate a certain code of behavior."[128]

But this tension between the individual and authority is not new. It has existed in Christianity at least since the Reformation, and Taylor laments that Christians have often forced people to extremes: "either utter self-suspicion or total self-trust."[129] Can't there be a middle ground? Taylor thinks so. Though he admits individualized experiences of the spiritual can often be feel-good and superficial, he doesn't think this is always the case. Indeed, he seems more sympathetic to the "spiritual quest" types than he does the conservatives who decry what they see as flimsy, undemanding spirituality:

> Some conservative souls feel that it is sufficient to condemn this age to note that it has led great numbers into modes of free-floating not very exigent spirituality. But they should ask themselves two questions: First, is it conceivable that one could return to a paleo- or even neo-Durkheimian dispensation? And, secondly, and more profoundly, doesn't every dispensation have its own favored forms of deviation? If ours tends to multiply somewhat shallow and undemanding spiritual options, we shouldn't forget the spiritual costs of various kinds of forced conformity: hypocrisy, spiritual stultification, inner revolt against the Gospel, the confusion of faith and power, and even worse. Even if we had a

---

127   Taylor, *A Secular Age*, 489.
128   Ibid., 508.
129   Ibid., 512.

choice, I'm not sure we wouldn't be wiser to stick with the present dispensation.[130]

In this section of A Secular Age, Taylor (like a true academic) complicates either/or dichotomies and suggests there can be many different iterations and assemblages of faith in this new spiritual landscape. But is he correct that the Age of Authenticity's free-floating, shallow, undemanding spirituality is simply a "deviation" of our present moment, no more problematic than any of the previous deviations in Christian history? Or is it a fundamental undermining of the gospel itself?

I believe it is the latter.

DISCIPLESHIP IS NOT CONSUMER-FRIENDLY

Christianity requires the submission of one's individual will to the lordship of Christ. It is impossible to simultaneously assert the sovereignty of one's subjective spiritual path and the supremacy of Jesus Christ. We are either in Christ on his terms and by his grace, or we aren't. Christianity doesn't work on the terms of consumerism. Jesus calls his followers not to comfort and convenience, but to deny themselves (Matt. 16:24) and take up their cross (Luke 14:27). Christian discipleship is not consumer-friendly. Further, Jesus calls us not to individualized, self-styled spirituality but to faith in community, accountable to others. Christianity disembedded from the church is not really Christianity. It feigns to embrace Jesus while shunning his body (see 1 Cor. 12, Eph. 1:22–23; 5:23; Col. 1:18).

Churches that attempt to accommodate the moving-target needs of individual "spiritual quests" are not doing

---

130   Taylor, A Secular Age, 512–13.

anyone a favor. By shifting the focus away from the fixed point of Jesus to the fickle, frequently diverging "paths" of individual churchgoers, churches lose their bearings and become inherently unstable. When a church becomes less about the demands of Scripture on individuals and more about the demands of individuals on the church to fit their preferences (favored music style, ideal sermon length, brand of coffee, and so on), it loses its power to transform us and subvert our idols. It becomes a commodity to be shopped for, consumed and then abandoned when another shinier, trendier, more "relevant" option appears.

This consumer framework also lends itself to weird mutations wherein bits and pieces of one church/tradition are combined with those of another, like a hipster might appropriate various disconnected motifs in assembling his personal style: the shoes of a Wall Street investor, the beard of a Canadian lumberjack, the Vineyard Vines button-downs of a Southern frat guy, the Persian tattoos of a Big Sur mystic, and so on.

In the same way, many spiritual seekers today (including many Christians) are "engaged in assembling their own personal outlook, through a kind of 'bricolage,'"[131] like spiritual flaneurs on some sort of ecclesiological Champs-Élysées. Perhaps they are passionately into Reformed theology but find Catholic art and liturgy beautiful. Or maybe they attend two or three churches simultaneously, opting for one or the other on any given Sunday, depending on their mood.

Can such an approach to eclectic faith, where spirituality is as customizable as a Spotify playlist or a Chipotle burrito, ever be conducive to spiritual health? Perhaps. In tempered forms and with deference to authority beyond the

---

131   Taylor, *A Secular Age*, 514.

self, a quirky hybrid Christianity can be orthodox. I know some deeply faithful Jesus-followers who define their current Christian identity in ways that defy rigid old boundaries (e.g. "Reformational Catholic" or "Reformed Charismatic"). And some of the healthiest and fastest-growing churches I've visited in recent years have been hybrids of various kinds (for example, Vintage Church: a charismatic Anglican church that merged with a Baptist church in Santa Monica, California).

There is a sense in which, in our forgetful and short-attention-span era, the "old" is easily made new again. Think of the way retro '80s synth music or "vintage" home decor trends have been repackaged as chic for the 21st century. Of course the "old" is never attractive holistically. A Brooklyn hipster may relish (and seek to replicate) great-grandmother's small-batch cookery and handmade DIY aesthetics, but not her religious piety or demure sense of domestic femininity. The same is true in today's post-Durkheimian faith landscape. Church shoppers might be simultaneously wowed by the "new" (new to them) aspects of Very Old Christianity (ancient creeds, Puritan hymns, the *Book of Common Prayer*, and so on) and resistant to the "old school" moral paradigms consistent in Christian history.

Churches should be aware of these eclectic tastes and recognize that the "old seeming new again" phenomenon can play to their advantage, insofar as it isn't a gimmick or marketing ploy. Christianity is both always old and always new, and that hybrid identity naturally resonates in today's restless spiritual landscape. A 21st-century church that has a beautifully designed website and celebrates the brilliance of Chance the Rapper—while also confessing the ancient creeds and underscoring the historical rootedness of liturgical practices—is likely to hold some appeal among today's church shoppers, who are always looking for a fresh combination of spiritual wisdom and mix-and-match church styles.

Yes, there are ways for churches to recognize and appeal to the eclectic appetites of the post-Durkheimian dispensation. But the key is to not do any of this in a reactive, "brand pivot" sort of way in response to the particular needs of this or that person, or because data show that liturgy plays well among millennials. Do it because it is reverent, not because it is relevant. Make sure you can communicate a compelling *why* behind your eclectic church style, beyond that it is "cool" or "beautiful" (or other such vagaries). Are your songs chosen in worship with low regard for lyrical depth and high regard for the "fresh sound" factor? Have you thought through the theological connotations of those vintage, ambience-setting Catholic prayer candles in your sanctuary? Does your congregation have a sense for the historical context and theological contours of the old-sounding creeds recited corporately in your Sunday services? These are some of the questions you might ponder as you examine whether your church's mix-and-match elements stem more from piecemeal pragmatism (audience-oriented relevance) than coherent worship (God-oriented reverence).

Relevance can coexist with reverence, but the former should always be a byproduct of the latter. The most relevant thing about a church is its deep reverence and contagious awe before the triune God. Pastors today should be mindful of what resonates broadly but not driven by the moving-target whims of the marketplace. They should be aware of the reality of church shoppers, but not always adjusting to fit the latest "consumer trend" or appeal to every church shopper's demand.

LORDSHIP OF CHRIST, NOT LORDSHIP OF CONSUMERS

It may be tempting for churches to "meet individual people where they are," celebrating and coming alongside the unique spiritual pilgrimages of every churchgoer. But this is unsustainable for the simple reason that people are all over the map. For a church to meet and affirm every congregant in his or her totally unique, individuated spirituality is to fragment in a hundred different directions, losing any sense of a beautiful, transcendent core that makes church matter in the first place. A better approach is to call the congregation, in its diversity, to meet Christ where *he* is, even if it means asking people to redirect or abandon their various self-defined spiritual paths. The lordship of Christ, not the lordship of consumers, should always hold sway.

Think about a sport declining in popularity. Maybe it's a sport that, in a certain culture, used to be ingrained: everyone grew up knowing, playing, and watching it together. It is just what you did. But now it's no longer a given most people enjoy the sport or even know how it's played. The social imaginary has changed enough that the sport no longer occupies a primary place in the average person's vision of the good life.

For those who love the sport and want to see it endure, some amount of adaptation to the changing culture will be in order. Perhaps the way the sport talks about itself changes, incorporating language and metaphors that appeal to the new social imaginary. Perhaps the technology used to broadcast or market the sport is updated.

But if the sport adapts itself too much to the gamut of what people want the game to be, soon enough it loses its original beauty entirely. By reworking the rules to fit the disparate desires of would-be players or audiences, the game loses its soul. Even the sport's faithful defenders lose interest.

This is what happens to churches whose weakened position in a secular age leads them to seek survival by assuming they must adjust to the restless whims and new spiritual paths of the "marketplace." It's an unsustainable approach for churches, because it's also a self-defeating path for churchgoers.

It's crucial for church and ministry leaders in a secular age to challenge themselves, and their congregations, to break out of this post-Durkheimian, expressive individualist approach to faith. It's a path to spiritual exhaustion and eventual death. Spiritual vitality, on the other hand, comes from embracing the necessity of being embedded within a larger structure—a church that provides support and accountability and draws us away from the dead-end prison of accountable-to-only-me spirituality.

On this point, Charles Taylor sounds a note of optimism when he describes how the "nagging dissatisfactions with the modern moral order" and the "continuing sense that there is something more" may lead people back to a more solid and stable religious community:

> The very fact that its forms are not absolutely in tune with much of the spirit of the age; a spirit in which people can be imprisoned, and feel the need to break out; the fact that faith connects us to so many spiritual avenues across different ages; this can over time draw people towards it.[132]

It is my hope that, in this Age of Authenticity, one of the prisons from which people will "feel the need to break out" is the self-defeating consumerism of subjective spiritual search-

---

132   Taylor, *A Secular Age*, 533.

ing. The suffocating interiority of true-to-yourself spirituality will, in the end, lead seekers to look beyond themselves. The question is whether they will not just *look* but *land* somewhere, settling down in an inevitably challenging church and setting aside their shopping lists.

8

POLITICS AND PUBLIC LIFE IN A SECULAR AGE

BRUCE RILEY ASHFORD

The contemporary era in Western civilization represents a radical desacralizing of the social order, unprecedented in human history. The German theologian Dietrich Bonhoeffer described it as a "world come of age," an era in which we have learned how to manage life without any reference to God.[133] American sociologist Philip Rieff referred to it as the third era in human history, an era in which sacred order has been severed from the social and cultural order, leaving Westerners without a matrix of meaning or an obligatory code of permissions and prohibitions.[134]

---

133   Dietrich Bonhoeffer, "Letter to Eberhard Bethge (June 8, 1944)," in Dietrich Bonhoeffer, *Letters and Papers from Prison*, Dietrich Bonhoeffer Works, vol. 8 (Minneapolis, MN: Fortress Press, 2010), 425–27.

134   Philip Rieff, *My Life among the Deathworks* (Charlottesville, VA: University of Virginia Press), 1–44.

But it is perhaps the Canadian philosopher Charles Taylor who, more than any other, has explored the implications of Western society's transition to a modern secular age. Although his analysis and evaluation can be found in a number of significant works, including *Sources of the Self*, *The Malaise of Modernity*, and *Modern Social Imaginaries*, it crystallizes and peaks in *A Secular Age*.[135]

Here he describes our secular age as one that considers belief in God implausible or unimaginable.[136] As modern Westerners, we live entirely within an "immanent" frame of reference. In the immanent frame, theistic belief not only been displaced from the default position, but is positively contested by myriad other options. It is merely one option among many—and an implausible and unimaginable one at that.

This new context brings with it a new "feel" in which theists and non-theists alike are haunted by doubt. Within the immanent frame, we search for meaning, and find an explosion of different options. As a result we are "fragilized"; surrounded by competing options in close proximity to ourselves, we lack confidence in our own beliefs. We are "cross-pressured"; caught between the modern disenchantment of the world and the haunting of transcendence, we find ourselves in perpetual unease.

But none of this would have happened, Taylor avers, without a political shift in which the West cast off strong

---

135 Charles Taylor, *Sources of the Self: The Making of Modern Identity* (Cambridge, MA: Harvard University Press, 1989); idem., *The Malaise of Modernity* (Toronto, ON: House of Anansi, 1991); idem., *Modern Social Imaginaries* (Durham, NC: Duke University Press, 2004); idem., *A Secular Age*.

136 Taylor, *A Secular Age*, 83.

forms of sacral authority and embraced a generic sort of "natural" religion. Natural religion was unencumbered by Christianity's code of permissions and prohibitions, and weakened or blocked out some of the ways Christianity had historically impinged on society and the public square.[137]

In a secular age such as ours, Taylor argues, Christians should avoid the error of secular humanists and Christian fundamentalists—namely, presenting our views with a smug condescension. Instead, we should present our faith humbly and sensitively to our cross-pressured and fragilized neighbors, suggesting that Christianity provides the key to human flourishing, moral transformation, and the unease caused by realities such as time and death. In short, we should allow Christian wisdom and virtue to animate our lives and shape our response.

Taylor's account of modernity is richly suggestive and helpful for Christians who recognize that the gospel is a public truth that therefore must be brought into an interface with secularized society and culture.[138] It's helpful in particular for Christians who wish to make Christianity "imaginable" again in Western politics and public life. Just as the West arrived at the current moment via a political shift in which the West desacralized the public square was sacral-

---

137   Taylor, A Secular Age, 234–42.
138   The gospel is a public truth in the sense that it announces publicly God's rule as king. The early church proclaimed the gospel in a way that exposed the Roman kingdom as a fraud. It is God through Jesus, not Rome via Caesar, who rules over all. See John Dickson, "Gospel as News: Euangel from Aristophanes to the Apostle Paul," New Testament Studies 51 (2005): 212–30; Lesslie Newbigin, Truth to Tell: The Gospel as Public Truth (Grand Rapids, MI: William B. Eerdmans, 1991).

ized, so must we move beyond this moment by appropriately resacralizing our involvement in public life.

Politics is the art of persuading our fellow citizens—including elected officials—about matters of common concern. As Christians, we want to "win over" others to our point of view on public matters. The gospel is a public truth, and we want it to prevail appropriately on public life. The early church preached the gospel in a way that sacralized the public square and exposed the Roman kingdom as a fraud. How can we do the same in our own context? How can we make the Christian gospel once again plausible and imaginable in our fragilized and cross-pressured era?

As Taylor argues, we cannot offer a merely intellectual remedy. If we wish to make the gospel once again imaginable in our liberal society, we must offer a storied community who embodies its truth. And the church is this community, whose confession and members can make Christianity imaginable again. It alone can reintroduce strong forms of sacral authority, offer a narrative that reimagines public life, reveal a code of permissions and prohibitions that can cause society to flourish, and cultivate the virtues and dispositions that speak to a fragilized and cross-pressured society.

CHURCH GATHERED AS ORGANIZED POLITICAL ASSEMBLY

In his essay "To Follow a Rule," Taylor expands on an allusion he makes in *A Secular Age* against intellectualist accounts of public life that view "reason giving" as the end-all and be-all for justifying our beliefs and persuading others. Following Wittgenstein and Bourdieu, he argues that "reason giving has a limit, and in the end must repose in another kind of understanding."[139] Especially in a fragilized and cross-pressured context, reason-giving must be placed on the background of active and adroit bodily engagement with others and the world.

Taylor's argument is consonant with biblical teaching that the local church is a community whose weekly gathering and liturgy embodies the gospel.[140] One ought not diminish the centrality of the local church for public witness. When Christ ascended in bodily form, he left a new community to embody the gospel for the good of the world. This community is intrinsically political as it assembles weekly, gathering around the confession that the risen and ascended Christ is King. It nourishes our Christian identity and sends us out as public witnesses to Christ's kingdom. It incubates the dispositions and virtues that advance the common good.[141]

---

139   Charles Taylor, "To Follow a Rule," in *Philosophical Investigations* (Cambridge, MA: Harvard University Press, 1995), 179. For a brief exploration of the connection Wittgenstein makes between epistemological justification and embodied communities, and the implications of this connection for theology, see Bruce Riley Ashford, "Wittgenstein's Theologians: A Survey of Ludwig Wittgenstein's Impact on Theology," *Journal of the Evangelical Theological Society* 50:2 (June 2007): 357–75.

140   James K. A. Smith, *Desiring the Kingdom: Worship, Worldview, and Cultural Formation* (Grand Rapids, MI: Baker, 2009), 131–214.

141   See James K. A. Smith's *Awaiting the King: Reforming Public Theology* (Grand Rapids, MI: Baker, forthcoming), which provides a corrective to the underemphasis on virtue in Reformed and evangelical accounts of politics and pluralism; John Inazu's account of "aspirational virtues" and "living speech" in *Confident Pluralism: Surviving and Thriving through Deep Difference* (Chicago, IL: University of Chicago Press, 2016), 83–103; and David Brooks's account of the connection between society

In this way the church serves as a formation center for public righteousness.[142]

The church should recognize that its political "power" is not found primarily in activism, but in its proclamation of the gospel—a proclamation that challenges the *cultus publicus* of any nation, including our American Empire. By proclaiming that Jesus is Lord (and, by implication, that Caesar is not), it nourishes our political identity and foreshadows the day when the King will return to install a one-party system and reconstitute the world under a reign of justice and peace.

Sunday morning public worship, then, prepares us for Monday morning public life.

CHURCH SCATTERED AS ORGANIC PUBLIC WITNESS

The church's political witness is rooted in the soil of the church's corporate worship, but branches out to bear fruit far beyond the corporate gathering. Our corporate confession of Jesus's lordship causes us to reimagine the political, reframe public issues, reform public dispositions, reshape political activism, and recover the lost art of persuasion. Each of these fruits nourishes a secular age starving for transcendence.[143]

Reimagining the Political

In *A Secular Age*, Taylor explores the complicated relation between Christianity and democratic liberalism in the West-

---

and character formation in *The Road to Character* (New York, NY: Random House, 2015).

142   Richard J. Mouw, *Political Evangelism* (Grand Rapids, MI: Eerdmans, 1973), 35–50.

143   Taylor, *A Secular Age*, 595.

ern political imagination. On the one hand, liberalism grew out of Christian belief and practice and continues to borrow capital from the Christian tradition. On the other hand, liberalism has increasingly distorted that tradition, even while drawing on it.[144]

Instead of positing an intrinsic antithesis between Christianity and liberal democracy, or between Christianity and any given modern political ideology, we should draw on the biblical narrative to help reshape the Western political imagination. God is always *sending* his people (e.g. Gen. 1; Matt. 28), preparing us to bring the gospel into an interface with new contextual realities. The church is always drawing us into worship to nourish our mission-political identity so that it can send us back into the world. Why would the disputed space of free markets, political elections, and public policies be an exception to our missional mandate?

In our secular age, therefore, we must cultivate the type of public witness that recovers the contours of the gospel's political vision—and then brings that vision into a "missionary encounter" with late-modern liberal democracy's political vision.[145] We must find compelling ways to show that the biblical narrative—rather than the narrative of our preferred political party, public intellectual, or media outlet—is the true story of the whole world.[146] We must be keen to identify

---

144 Taylor, *A Secular Age*, 234–59.
145 This point is integral to James K. A. Smith's thesis in *Awaiting the King* (Grand Rapids, MI: Baker, forthcoming).
146 Lesslie Newbigin, "Evangelism in the Context of Secularization," in *The Study of Evangelism: Exploring a Missional Practice of the Church*, P.W. Chilcote, L.C. Warner, eds. (Grand Rapids, MI: Eerdmans, 2008), 46–55.

the idols that haunt modern political ideologies.[147] We must make clear, not only through spoken word but also through embodied habit, that our political affiliations and commitments are tentative in light of our allegiance to Christ. We are a people who believe occupants to Caesar's throne come and go, but Jesus remains forever.

Reframing Public Issues and Reforming Public Dispositions

Taylor describes the value our secular age places on human flourishing, yet notes that the secular vision for flourishing is stunted, having no transcendent source and no further purpose. In fact, an increasing number of public intellectuals do not merely lack a transcendent source; they urge our society to view "transcendent" morality as something that poisons society and undermines human flourishing.

In response, the Christian community has an opportunity to show how Christianity's transcendent vision not only provides the context within which society can flourish, but how it also does so better than rival visions. Following the lead of patristic fathers such as Augustine and modern intellectuals such as Groen van Prinsterer and Abraham Kuyper, we can argue theologically and philosophically that the "immanent frame" always and necessarily absolutizes some aspect of created reality and, in so doing, distorts cultural institutions and deforms society. We can substantiate our arguments by drawing on social scientists such as Philip Rieff and Robert Putnam to explore the ruinous effects of the

---

147   For an exploration of the idolatrous tendencies of modern Western political ideologies, see David T. Koyzis, *Political Visions and Illusions: A Survey & Critique of Contemporary Ideologies* (Grand Rapids, MI: IVP, 2002).

"immanent frame" on specific cultural institutions and social goods such as marriage and family, sexuality, art, literature, education, and the economy.

Additionally, we can explore crippling effects of the "immanent frame" on the notion of public morality itself. Historically, all societies have justified moral codes by means of an outside source, but in an unprecedented move, modern Western society has reduced morality to self-authorization.[148] This brings about an ironic situation: our secular age is increasingly concerned with moral permissions and prohibitions, but decreasingly able to justify them.[149] This causes problems politically both in terms of public policy-making and civil demeanor, as citizens cannot articulate *why* "the other" should submit to their self-authorized moral code. Taylor calls this the "extraordinary inarticulacy of modern culture."[150] Referring to this inarticulacy, Tim Keller writes that we find ourselves in a situation in which "all we can do is shout the other person down."[151]

Finally, in a public square in which citizens are shouting each other down, we must build churches and communities that incubate Christian virtue. For example, Taylor bemoans the egocentric disposition fostered by our secular age—a disposition of "mutual display" and "confident smugness" in which we use every medium available to express ourselves loudly so others will overhear.[152] In response, the church, by God's grace, can inculcate in us a cruciform disposition of

---

148   Taylor, *A Secular Age*, 580–89.
149   Ibid., 605–06.
150   Charles Taylor, *The Malaise of Modernity* (Toronto: House of Anansi Press Limited, 1991), 18.
151   Timothy Keller, *Making Sense of God*, 180.
152   Taylor, *A Secular Age*, 473–95.

humility in which we use our gifts and resources to serve and empower others. If our Lord—the King of the universe—was willing to serve as a homeless itinerant teacher whose life was crushed on a cross, then we can be willing to work on behalf of persons and groups who are financially disadvantaged, ethnically downtrodden, or socially marginalized. If our Lord turned the other cheek to his tormenters, then we can refuse to respond in kind when we are mocked, demeaned, purposely misrepresented, or demonized.

Reshaping Political Activism and Recovering the Lost Art of Persuasion

Over the course of the past half-century, many American evangelicals have put their eggs in the basket of short-term political activism—with the emphasis on the *political* and the *short-term*. Often operating out of what Taylor calls a Secular[1] or Secular[2] mentality, we reduced culture to politics, and politics to short-term activism, assuming a large part of the remedy to our social and cultural ills lies in a quick political fix.[153] Repeatedly, we've treated each presidential election or mid-term election as the one that—despite all historical evidence to the contrary—will finally deliver our hopes and ease our fears.

---

153   In Taylor's taxonomy of our secular age, Secular[1] represents the Classical/Medieval era, in which "secular" is the opposite of "sacred," and represents the temporal realm instead of the heavenly. Secular[2] refers to the Enlightenment era in which the notion of "secular" refers to a purportedly neutral or non-sectarian standpoint. Secular[3] refers to our current cross-pressured and fragilized era in which all religious belief is contestable and any particular religious view is merely one option among many.

In response, the Christian community needs to draw on Kuyper and others to cast a vision in which culture is not reduced to politics. We should take the broad view of cultural influence by working faithfully to renew every dimension of culture—not merely politics, but marriage, family, art, science, business, and education. Our political witness—especially in a Secular³ context—will gain plausibility from a unified and faithful presence in society's many spheres. Additionally, we need to play the long game by not putting all of our hopes in short-term power political power plays. Short-term activism has its place, but its ability to shape society and culture is limited, and it can tempt us to sacrifice long-term witness on the altar of short-term political gain.

As we take the broad view of culture and play the long game of sustainable public witness, we are seeking to recover, as Os Guinness puts it, "the lost art of Christian persuasion." In the decades and centuries immediately after our Lord's ascension, the church used two symbols for the art of Christian advocacy: the closed fist and the open hand. The closed fist represented *dissuasoria*, the negative side of apologetics that defends against attack. The open hand represented *persuasoria*, the positive side of apologetics that uses intellectual, aesthetic, and relational creativity in defense of the gospel. "Expressing the love and compassion of Jesus, and using eloquence, creativity, imagination, humor, and irony, open-hand apologetics had the task of helping to pray open hearts and minds that, for a thousand reasons, had long grown resistant to God's great grace, so that it could shine like the sun."[154]

---

154   Os Guinness, *Fool's Talk: Recovering the Lost Art of Christian Persuasion* (Downers Grove, IL: IVP, 2015), 253.

We must regain this lost art of persuasion in the midst of our radically unprecedented cross-pressured and fragilized age. Lesslie Newbigin's exhortation is prescient:

> [T]he call to the Church is to enter vigorously into the struggle for truth in the public domain. We cannot look for the security which would be ours in a restored Christendom. Nor can we continue to accept the security which is offered in an agnostic pluralism. . . . We are called, I think, to bring our faith into the public arena, to publish it, to put it at risk in the encounter with other faiths and ideologies in open debate and argument, and in the risky business of discovering what Christian obedience means in radically new circumstances and in radically human cultures.[155]

We must embrace the moment God has given us—a secularized, cross-pressured, fragilized moment. When the Lord returns, we will meet him first and foremost as Christians. But we will also meet him as citizens of the modern West. Being a cross-pressured and fragilized Westerner is not the most important dimension of our identity, but it is an unavoidable one for which we will give account. For that reason, it is incumbent on us to tailor our witness for a secular age.

---

155   Lesslie Newbigin, *Truth to Tell: The Gospel as Public Truth* (Grand Rapids, MI: William B. Eerdmans, 1991), 59.

9

FREE FAITH: INVENTING NEW WAYS OF BELIEVING AND LIVING TOGETHER

GREG FORSTER

Religious freedom is reshaping the world. While precious, it has come with a high cost. Historically, all our forms of social order—political, economic, familial, ecclesial, and social—assumed that society would share a religion, or at least a metaphysic and worldview. So they have all been undermined by the pluralism that religious freedom permits. And we have not yet figured out how to build new forms of social order that will be stable and just without enforcing orthodoxy.

Without a common god, we lack a common good. That is the first challenge. It is hard to find shared moral ground on which to build a way of living in peace with each other. This is why worldliness and strife are increasing in our communities.

But there is a second and deeper challenge. Religious freedom brings with it a different way of experiencing religion itself. It destabilizes all religious positions—not just fidelity to this or that religion but even belief and unbelief simply as such. It is harder now to be a really committed Christian, or even a really committed theist; it is also, in a different way, harder to be a really committed atheist. Our chaotic cultural environment undermines the sources of moral character and intellectual confidence. The only thing that has become easier (at least in the short term) is therapeutic deism and being "spiritual but not religious"—passively surrendering to each spiritual mood as it happens along.

The challenge of advanced modernity is not simply that Christians stand here and atheists stand there, and we lack common ground. It has also gotten much harder for anyone to stand on any ground.

As our religious, political, economic, and social crises increase, more people realize that confronting this challenge is not optional for either the church or the nations. The church's crisis of discipleship (we have millions of Christians whose daily lives look the same as everyone else's) and the crisis of public virtue and solidarity in our nations (public communities that are materialistic, polarized, and degenerating) have a common root. Growing strong in the faith and living in peace with our neighbors both require us to invent new ways of living for the new world religious freedom has created.

To effectively evangelize, disciple, and do justice and mercy, we must embrace anew the modern commitment to religious freedom. But we must embrace it as our early modern ancestors did—as an uncompleted project, aimed at discovering solutions to an unsolved problem. It is hard to admit ignorance. But if we admit that the project of religious freedom is incomplete and the problem unsolved, we can overcome the paralysis that otherwise threatens to overwhelm the church.

HISTORY HAS PRODUCED A NEW RELIGIOUS CONSCIOUSNESS

Most American evangelicals frame the problem something like this: The church is basically the same as it ever was (it follows the same gospel, after all), but the world has suddenly and inexplicably gone mad. The fallen world was always dysfunctional, but it used to be dysfunctional in relatively routine and predictable ways. Now it is totally haywire. Fortunately, we have social scientists and philosophers and other professional smart people to tell us why the world went crazy and hand us a well-developed set of solutions we can implement.

Here is a better frame: Christianity in the advanced modern world faces enormous new challenges, and also enormous new opportunities, because religious freedom is transforming every kind of social structure. Religious freedom and modern ways of viewing the world are deeply interdependent, and have destabilized not only the social order but even religion itself. They have produced a new kind of religious consciousness. Religion is now something different, for believers and unbelievers alike. We do not yet understand our new situation well enough to know how to cope with these changes—individually, or as a church, or as nations. The only viable option is to trust God through the infallible Bible and the supernatural transformation of the Holy Spirit to lead us, like Abram, out into the wilderness.

We are sojourning to a new land. Where we are going is known to God, but not yet to us—not even to the social scientists and philosophers and professional smart people.

Evangelicals cheer when you say we must trust God through the infallible Bible and the supernatural transformation of the Holy Spirit. But they march with torches and pitchforks if you dare to talk about historical changes having brought about a new kind of religious consciousness.

The evangelical movement as we know it was formed in a reaction against "modernist" theologies that overemphasized Keeping Up with History at the expense of fidelity to eternal truth, so evangelicals have long been suspicious of historical consciousness.

I am heartened, however, by increasing signs that we are discovering the importance of history. Among evangelical leaders, 50 years' worth of complex scholarly discussion of modernity and religion is at last beginning to get a serious hearing. "Unknown unknowns" are becoming "known unknowns." Taylor's *A Secular Age* has been an important source for that conversation, as have Lesslie Newbigin's works, Dallas Willard's *The Divine Conspiracy*, James Davison Hunter's *To Change the World*,[156] Peter Berger's *The Many Altars of Modernity*, and others. It's even becoming possible to hope that someday soon we will start taking the Niebuhr brothers seriously again.

IMMANENT FRAME RESHAPES OUR UNIVERSE

Central to Taylor's book is the concept of the immanent frame—a certain way of looking at the world of daily experience. It interprets all phenomena we encounter in the world *other than the activity of human minds* as explainable by mechanistic natural causes. The exclusion of the human mind from the domain of natural causes (which is accepted by all but a few hardcore materialists) is important. The immanent frame presents us with a fully explainable natural world, but also

---

156   See Collin Hansen, ed., *Revisiting 'Faithful Presence'*: To Change the World *Five Years Later* (Deerfield, IL: The Gospel Coalition, 2015). https://www.thegospelcoalition.org/article/revisiting-faithful-presence-to-change-the-world-five-years-later

with a sense of ourselves as existing separate from that world and also from the supernatural world. Our consciousness becomes what Taylor calls a "buffered self" rather than a "porous self."

The immanent frame can be held in a way that is "open" to the supernatural (i.e., we see supernatural causes at work in our world, working behind and through natural causes). Or it can be "closed" (i.e., we hold that natural causes are the only forces at work in the natural world). The existence of the immanent frame makes secularism possible as a stable and publicly legitimized way of life, but it does not compel secularism.

Before modernity, seeing the world through the immanent frame was so implausible that it was for practical purposes impossible to live with that mindset. All public and social institutions were built on the assumption that the world of daily experience is suffused with many kinds of supernatural operations—working not behind and through natural causes but independently, excluding natural explanations.

Today, everyone—the Christian, the Muslim, the Hindu, the atheist and the wishy-washy Spiritual But Not Religionist alike—sees the world through the immanent frame. People have many different ways of understanding the thinking, feeling, and willing of the human mind, ranging from the image of God to Darwinian algorithms to the divine spark of Brahmin metaphysics. But everyone agrees about why water flows downhill and electrical current follows the path of least resistance and water boils at 212 degrees Fahrenheit. They do this because Isaac Newton commands them to.

The immanent frame empowers us for all the blessings of modernity, and inflicts all its woes on us as well. It is indispensable to modern science and rapid technological progress. It also provides a common social world that facilitates peace among peoples of different nations and religions, and the harmony that makes economic prosperity possible. It also drains the ordinary world of its deepest moral and spiritual significance, consigning not only atheists but also Christians and everyone else to struggle to find real meaning and purpose in their everyday lives. Worldliness becomes easier, feeding both cynicism and fanaticism.

'REFORM' AND RELIGIOUS FREEDOM CREATE AND SUSTAIN THE IMMANENT FRAME

Why did it take so long for the immanent frame to emerge, and why did every civilization on earth resist it for so long? Secularists tell a "subtraction story," in which the irrationality of religious belief and the cynical use of religion for social control were all that ever stood in the way of the immanent frame. Then along came the Reason Fairy to sprinkle Enlightenment Dust on our heads; religion was subtracted from the picture, and the immanent frame naturally emerged. Taylor debunks this story at some length.

Instead, he blames the spirit of Reform. The capitalized "Reform" is distinct from "reform." The former seeks comprehensive innovation and improvement across the whole canvas of human experience and social organization, while the latter seeks marginal improvements and treats the basic structure of human institutions as natural and permanent.

To sum up Taylor's complex argument briefly: In primitive religions around the world, our drives for immoral forms of violence and sexuality were accepted and normalized. Religious rituals provided a socially legitimate outlet to contain them. These religions were interdependent with the porous self; there was not much boundary between the mind, the body, the natural world, and the supernatural. To see the world as something to be manipulated and controlled by us (i.e., the immanent frame) requires a buffered self that conceives of "the world" and "us" as radically separate things. This was simply not how the ancient mind understood itself.

As mature religions emerged worldwide in what is known as the "Axial age" in the first millennium B.C., religious rituals that incorporated our lust for vengeance and obscenity were condemned. People now aspired to levels of self-discipline, compassion, and dignity that would eliminate immoral violence and sex rather than ritualize them. This produced a new mindset—a new way of understanding both ourselves and our world—that ultimately became the spirit of Reform. And as we sought more and more control over our world in order to Reform it, the immanent frame emerged, along with the buffered self: minds that experience the world as something radically separate from themselves.

There is much to commend this account. However, with Berger, I would emphasize the special role of religious freedom in producing the immanent frame in its fully developed form. For one thing, this account is enormously helpful in explaining why the immanent frame emerged with such enormous force in Europe, at the specific time it did, and spread elsewhere from there (through both colonization and persuasion) rather than developing indigenously in every part of the world. Taylor himself emphasizes—and is careful to clearly condemn—the role of the Reformation as the supreme exemplar of the spirit of Reform.

It is true, as Taylor relates, that the spirit of Reform helped produce the religious division of Europe in the Reformation. People like Luther and Calvin and the Radical Reformers were prepared to overthrow even the greatest and most important social structures, if it was the right thing to do. They did not take the empire and the papacy to be natural, permanent features of human life.

However, it is also true that once the religious division of the Reformation proved intractable, the spirit of Reform turned right around and produced an unexpected remedy: religious freedom. It was Christ's cause of justice and mercy—the spirit of Reform—that demanded we learn to live in peace with one another. At first we made civil peace among Christians, then with those of all faiths, and finally with those of no faith. Eventually, a whole new kind of social order had to be invented to accommodate this demand for living in peace together; we are still in the process of inventing it.

This stage was essential to the final development of the immanent frame, and remains essential today to its continuing social dominance. We cannot live in peace with one another if our mental universes are totally different. Religious freedom therefore created a drive to find a shared way of speaking and acting together in public spaces with those of other beliefs.

To borrow an example from Berger, the Christian pilot and the atheist co-pilot need a shared discourse (i.e., a common mode of communication) if they're going to fly the plane through a storm together. The pilot believes that the storm might be turned aside through prayer. He may pray silently, but he can't bring prayer into the shared discourse with his co-pilot. They *need* an immanent frame; they can't fly the plane without it.

Once the presence of religious plurality becomes normalized, the immanent frame must be normalized with it. At that point, even if the pilot and co-pilot are both Christians, it will not feel normal or natural for them to pray together in the flight deck.

FREEDOM AND FRAGMENTATION

It is important to see what a dramatic difference this makes to the way we organize society. In every time and place around the world, the porous self is associated with what

Taylor calls "complementary hierarchies." Kings, priests, landowners, scholars and artists rule the roost, while ordinary people must do—and think—whatever they are told by their betters. If each individual self is just one more atom in the great cosmos, then who cares about it? It is only with the buffered self that individuals begin to matter. In modernity, and only in modernity, we find social orders based (in principle) on an ethic of equality and freedom.

From a slightly different angle, one can describe the change in modernity in terms of "differentiation"—the disentanglement, and eventually dissociation, of political, economic, religious, familial, educational, artistic, and other structures from one another. An ancient Greek would have been utterly baffled to hear you attempt to explain the distinction between religion and politics; he knew that the king and the priest had different functions, but both of their roles were what we would call "religious," and both were also "political." If he ever really grasped the distinction you were trying to draw, he would either laugh at you or cut your throat. For medieval Europe, the distinction between religion and politics was palpably present, and the unquiet frontier between king and pope was a source of great tension; but this tension arose precisely because religion and politics, though now distinct, were seen as inextricably interdependent. Today, the question is whether there is any way we can relate them to each other at all without becoming monsters.

This change is what makes the modern world so beautiful and so terrible. It is this, and only this, that has abolished slavery and torn down horrible tyrannies, liberated women and empowered economic development, opened new doors of ethnic coexistence, protected religious minorities from persecution, and protected religious majorities from the corruptions of power. And this change has also left us awash in cultural chaos, struggling to form stable beliefs or deep moral character, polarized and perpetually fighting, unable to say with certainty what anything means in the public square (as opposed to what it means to me, or to my social faction).

We should never regret the rise of religious freedom. All other social orders, from Rome to Stalin, have been built on whips and torture chambers. From time to time I meet people who have picked up little fragments of *A Secular Age*, and they say things like, "We have to figure out how to get rid of the buffered self and get back to the porous self." These people simply don't know what they're asking for. God help them if they ever have occasion to find out.

However, as Hunter has described with penetrating insight, the pluralistic social environment permitted by religious freedom does lead to a "dissolution" of the shared meanings of words. Moral consensus and peaceful resolution of conflicts become ever more difficult. And there are rich rewards for those who know how to mobilize mass resentments.

One thing is for sure: There is no going back. The economic and technological development of the modern world creates what Berger calls "epistemic contagion." In a world of rapid transit and instant communication, you simply can't avoid the pluralistic social environment. Various kinds of fundamentalism—religious and secular—may attempt to create homogeneous social environments; not only do they fail and collapse, but even while they last they never really establish the epistemically pure mindset they seek. Fundamentalist social worlds exist only as a reaction against pluralism, and a continual consciousness of pluralism is essential to their structure.

The greatest barrier to any kind of reversal of the immanent frame is the specifically religious effect of epistemic contagion. Back when people lived in social environments that were small, homogenous, and isolated, it was possible for people to take their religious beliefs for granted. Today, belief of any kind *must* be a conscious choice, and that fact changes everything about it.

One of the most prominent changes this creates is that religious coercion becomes impossible and even absurd. In any environment with epistemic contagion, the use of power to impose religion becomes self-discrediting and therefore self-defeating. The great Christian leader J. Gresham Machen summed up the case for religious freedom succinctly: "It is quite useless to approach a man with both a club and an argument."

UNDISCOVERED COUNTRY OF RELIGIOUS FREEDOM

If there is no going back, our job is to get busy inventing new forms of religious formation and social order that can function in the new environment. More than likely, you and I will not live to see the results of this endeavor. Our job is not to invent the future but to put the church in the right position to do so. We will have succeeded if our children grow up understanding that religious freedom was, from the beginning, an *experiment*—and that modernity only went wrong when it forgot this fact.

What does that endeavor involve? Here are my suggestions:

First, embrace religious freedom wholeheartedly, and accept that the challenges of the advanced modern world are the price we pay for that freedom. We must not only sacrificially support the religious-freedom rights of our non-Christian neighbors, but also rejoice to do so; every Christian should be prepared sacrifice whatever it takes—to die if necessary—to protect our neighbors' right not to believe. And we must face cultural chaos with courage and hope. It is an iron law of human affairs that you cannot reform something if you don't love it. The more ardently you love the modern world, the more power you will have to reform it.

Second, accept the frightening and humbling fact that we don't already possess a solution to the problems of advanced modernity. We must learn to identify and expose, under its many devious guises, our unconscious refusal to reckon with that fact. In politics, this unconscious refusal is one reason we emphasize mobilizing our own power to defeat our enemies rather than seeking out new coalitions for doing justice and mercy. In churches, it feeds spiritual complacency; religion becomes a consumer product without transformative power. We can't get busy finding a solution until we really accept that we don't know the solution already.

Third, be more intentional about building Christian communities that are distinct and formative as Christian communities, but whose purpose is bringing the holy love of God *out of* those communities and into an unholy world. Local churches are at the center, and every kind of association where Christians gather to equip each other is important. If we are not intentional about building distinctly Christian communities, our identity and mission will get lost in the shifting cultural sands. But those communities must not exist for the sake of maintaining our own identity and mission. Christian communities ought to exist to bring the holy love of God to our neighbors in word and action. Real spiritual formation is mobilization for a mission, not narcissistic navel-gazing.

Fourth, build moral consensus in the public square and seek what Berger calls "formulas of peace" with those of different convictions. If we believe in religious freedom, it is incumbent on us to find ways of living in peace. This starts with building moral consensus. What we need is not a mere truce (i.e., I won't hit you if you don't hit me) but real areas of moral agreement and shared values (i.e., hitting people is wrong). And such agreement does not exist naturally in a pluralistic social environment; it will exist only if we are intentional about building it.

That will already be happening if we have followed the steps outlined above. If we are seeking out ways to serve our communities and live godly lives in the present evil age, we will already be at work discovering and exposing areas of potential moral progress in our culture. Faithful discipleship applied to everyday life produces opposition from worldly powers, but it attracts many of the lost. Diligent efforts by the church to put God's holy love into action in the unholy world create conflict, as they did in the Reformation; but they tend to culminate, as they did in the Reformation, in new formulas of peace that co-opt the fruit of the church's labor and make it part of the social order.

The rise of religious freedom has uprooted virtually everything we used to take for granted in our social world. That's because older social orders were so horribly unjust that religious freedom's ethic of equality and freedom tore up their very roots. If we are living through a period of chaos today, let's be grateful we aren't living under the stability of what came before. And if building moral consensus seems like a daunting task, what shall we say to the martyrs who were executed by torture simply for preaching the Word?

Let God's church receive the blessings of religious freedom with gratitude, and receive the challenges of our moment in history as God's provision for our sanctification and for the advance of his glory in our nations.

10

WHOSE WILL BE DONE? HUMAN FLOURISHING IN THE SECULAR AGE

JEN POLLOCK MICHEL

She called it a "selective reduction." Describing to me years of failed infertility treatments, my friend relived the grief of barrenness. Even after she and her husband began attempting in vitro fertilization, she bled disappointment and shed hope with every new month.

The desire for children became more urgent; the doctor, more reckless. After several failed attempts, he assured my friend and her husband that their chance of multiples was quite low and implanted a handful of fertilized eggs. Four "took." Four babies with pulsing hearts began growing in that once-hostile womb.

Seeds to become saplings to become trees.

When the doctor delivered the news, it was not the scene of Gabriel's annunciation. The doctor insisted that my friend either "selectively reduce" two of the fetuses or face the possibility that none survived. Though she had spent a childhood of Sundays on kneelers, a lifetime praying the "Our Father," my friend was not prepared for the collision of wills: the divine will to sanctify life, the human will to manage the odds.

My friend's twins are beautiful, healthy children.

New Yorker writer Margaret Talbot remembers her own abortion as a college freshmen at U.C. Berkeley, but without my friend's palpable regret.[157] Writing to counter the guilt women feel in seeking a "safe, legal medical procedure," Talbot calls her decision to "end a pregnancy" one of the most consequential decisions of her young life. "It allowed me to claim the future I imagined for myself." At 18, she describes having neither the wisdom for motherhood nor the fortitude for adoption, although later in her 30s she did begin a family with a supportive husband. "In some foundational way," Talbot muses with gratitude, "I have my abortion to thank for that."

To further the idea of abortion as "social and *moral* good" (emphasis mine), Talbot cites the work of Willie Parker, an abortion provider and "follower of Jesus." Parker believes abortion to be a deeply ethical choice made by parent(s) whose desire for a child is the only thing to imbue it with sacredness. Parker explains, "As a free human being, you are allowed to change your mind, to find yourself in different circumstances, to make mistakes. *You are allowed to want your own future.*" Parker sees dignity in his patients' desire to exercise their freedom, holiness in his call to grant their choice.

As he writes in his book, *Life's Work,* "The procedure room in an abortion clinic is as sacred as any other space to me. . . . In this moment, where you need something

---

157   Margaret Talbot, "Why It's Become So Hard to Get an Abortion," *New Yorker*, April 3, 2017.

that I am trained to give you, God is meeting both of us where we are."[158]

MY WILL BE DONE

These stories do not represent a singular experience of abortion. My friend ultimately followed her doctor's advice, but her tears bore witness to moral injury and regret. Margaret Talbot triumphantly invoked the "all-trumping argument" to defend her abortion: *choice.*[159] (As Charles Taylor would note, she fails to mention the "sacrificed alternatives in a dilemmatic situation, and the real moral weight of the situation."[160]) Of the three, Willie Parker is the most enigmatic. We understand abortion as regret, abortion as choice.

But abortion as *worship*?

It is tempting, like Chicken Little, to decry the abasement of morality in contemporary culture, especially when compared (however naively) to an idyllic yesteryear. The sky is falling! Defense of abortion and headlines like, "Bestselling Female Author Divorces Husband and Marries Woman!" reinforce the perception of our age as being driven by a newer, crasser breed of self-interest.

My will be done.

But as Taylor argues, it is not that the secular age has no spiritual or moral shape, no spiritual or moral aspiration. Godlessness does not inevitably produce moral fecklessness. In fact, in the 21st century, we're asking the same urgent questions people have always asked: "What constitutes a fulfilled life? What makes life really worth living? What would we

---

158   Quoted in Talbot, "Why It's Become So Hard to Get an Abortion."
159   Charles Taylor, *A Secular Age*, 478.
160   Ibid., 479.

most admire people for?"[161] Unbelievers, like believers, want to live well—and not simply for the temporary, tickling pleasures of base desires. "We strive to live happily with spouse and children, while practicing a vocation we find fulfilling, and also which constitutes an obvious contribution to human welfare."[162] According to Taylor, the fundamental shift of the secular age isn't declining belief in God or waning ethical commitments. It lies in our definition of "fullness."

If death is coming for us all, how do we make this "one wild and precious life" count?[163]

LET HUMANS FLOURISH

In primitive tribal societies, "gods" were a given feature of the landscape. While they might have been alternatively benevolent or hostile, they did not necessarily demand self-renunciation for the sake of otherworldly devotion. One offered sacrifices to the gods, yes. But the sacrifices sought temporal benefit. "What the people ask for when they invoke or placate divinities and powers is prosperity, health, long life, fertility; what they ask to be preserved from is disease, dearth, sterility, premature death."[164] The desires and aspirations of "early religion" were deeply rooted in a vision of the good life, here and now.

Let humans flourish.

By contrast, later religions, like Christianity, invoke higher goals for human flourishing than good harvests and

---

161   Taylor, *A Secular Age*, 16.
162   Ibid., 7.
163   Mary Oliver, "The Summer Day," in *Mary Oliver: New and Selected Poems* (Boston: Beacon, 1992), 94.
164   Taylor, *A Secular Age*, 150.

healthy babies. "There is a notion of our good which goes beyond human flourishing, which we may gain even while failing utterly on the scales of human flourishing, even *through* failing (like dying young on a cross) . . . [Christianity] redefines our ends so as to take us beyond flourishing."[165] In the example of Christianity, when God entered history, clothing himself with flesh to die a humiliating, degrading death by crucifixion, we have a shift in the sense of divine demand. God might not only purpose my happiness—he actually might, mysteriously, will that I suffer. As Taylor aptly notes, at the cross of Jesus Christ there stands an irreducible difference between the injunction "Thy will be done" and "Let humans flourish."

Modern exclusive humanism returns us to the mode of early religion (if also taking us a step further by eliminating the notion of "god"). "A way of putting our present condition," Taylor writes, "is to say that many people are happy living for goals which are purely immanent; they live in a way that takes no account of the transcendent."[166] In the secular age, "cross-pressured" as we are between doubt and belief, we can't know for certain if God exists. But if he does, surely he wills our good.

Which betrays the real problem: secularism is not the problem "out there." Instead, every Sunday morning, it is "secular" people filling our pews. They attest to loving Jesus—but accept "no final goals beyond human flourishing, nor any allegiance to anything else beyond this flourishing."[167] They pray for God's kingdom to come—and imagine the advent of their own happiness.

––––––––––––

165   Taylor, *A Secular Age*, 151.
166   Ibid., 143.
167   Ibid., 18.

In the secular age, God becomes the guarantor of *our best life now*.

THE GOOD LIFE AND THE MAXIMAL DEMAND

Through Scripture, we see the goodness of God in his extravagant will to *give*. As the curtain opens on creation, his first command is not prohibition but invitation: "Be fruitful and multiply." When the people of Israel are poised to enter the Promised Land, Moses sets before them the alternatives of "life and good, death and evil," and reprises God's creation invitation: "Live and multiply and the LORD your God will bless you in the land that you are entering" (Deut. 30:16). The gospel itself climaxes in God's giving: "For God so loved the world that he *gave*."

But with the cross at the center of Christianity, critics have suggested that God opposes our flourishing—that obedience is not a means to the good life but rather a form of masochism. As Jesus himself said, in the kingdom of God the only way to save one's life is to lose it first.

For modern secularists, there is the sense that Christianity has made exaggerated moral demands, which "cannot but end up mutilating us; it leads us to despise and neglect the ordinary fulfillment and happiness which is within our reach."[168] It asks us to despise our families (Luke 14:26); it commends heavenly treasure over earthly accumulation (Matt. 6:19); it forbids sexual license (Heb. 13:4). According to the critique, Christianity imposes a cruel and unnecessary asceticism, forcing us to repress desire and offending the primacy of individual freedom, the heartbeat of modern exclusive humanism.

---

168   Taylor, *A Secular Age*, 623–624.

It is not simply that Christianity is an alternate ethic in the secular age; it is an enemy.

"In recent centuries, and especially the last one, countless people have thrown off what has been presented to them as the demands of religions, and have seen themselves as rediscovering the value of the ordinary human satisfactions that these demands forbade. They had the sense of coming back to a forgotten good, a treasure buried in everyday life."[169] In other words, humanity flourishes by throwing off the deadening constraints of religion and following the whims of their desires—wherever those desires might lead.

To illustrate this point, Taylor talks about French writer André Gide's coming out in the 1920s. It was a "move in which desire, morality and a sense of integrity came together. . . . It is not just that Gide no longer feels the need to maintain a false front; it is that after a long struggle he sees this front as a wrong that he is inflicting on himself, and on others who labor under similar disguises."[170] Seen from the value-laden perspective of the secular age, Gide does not abandon moral commitments so much as take them up, courageously choosing to live as his most authentic self. Gide is one of many to declare his only binding moral demand to be, "Find yourself, realize yourself, release your true self."[171] His (and ours) is an Age of Authenticity, wherein there are no rules to keep except the dictates of personal desire.

As one popular author—a self-proclaimed follower of Jesus—baldly put it when defending a new lesbian relationship,

---

169   Taylor, *A Secular Age*, 627.
170   Ibid., 475.
171   Ibid., 475.

"The most revolutionary thing a woman can do is not explain herself."[172]

CRUCIFORM LIFE

How can we give ourselves fully to earth and heaven at the same time? Sure, personal fulfillment and piety may be compatible, but as Taylor observes, "The tension between fulfillment and dedication to God is still very much unresolved in our lives."[173] In the Middle Ages, the solution for resolving this tension was a division of labor: the kingdom of heaven was furthered in the celibate vocations, the kingdom of earth by everyone else. But insofar as the Reformation abolished the sacred/secular divide, it did not fundamentally resolve the tension.

> For the ordinary householder this answer seems to require something paradoxical: living in all the practices and institutions of flourishing, but at the same time not fully in them. Being in them but not of them; being in them, but yet at a distance, ready to lose them.[174]

How can we, as Dietrich Bonhoeffer described in a letter to his fiancée, say yes to God *and* yes to God's earth?[175]

---

172   When Glennon Doyle Melton announced on Facebook that she was dating Abby Wambach, she took up the impenetrable moral defense of the secular age: authenticity.

173   Taylor, *A Secular Age*, 656.

174   Ibid., 81.

175   In a letter to his fiancée from his prison cell, Bonhoeffer writes, "Our marriage must be a 'yes' to God's earth . . . I fear that Christians who venture to stand on earth on only one leg will stand in heaven on only one leg too."

We can't ignore Calvary at the center of our story, an irrefutable symbol of self-sacrifice. The cross is not just a "merely regrettable byproduct of a valuable career of teaching," and it will always challenge our instinctive ideas about flourishing.[176] On the one hand, Taylor assures readers that Jesus's agony at the moment of his death upholds the dignity of bodily life. "It is precisely because human life is so valuable, part of the plan of God for us, that giving it up has the significance of a supreme act of love."[177] On the other, even bodily life is something we should willing to lose at any moment.

Perhaps, as my pastor has suggested, we might imagine the life of faith standing on the knife edge of the Lord's Prayer salutation: Our *Father* in heaven, *hallowed* be your name. God is a good Father, and as Calvin wrote, this "frees us from all mistrust." But he is also holy. There's inscrutability to his ways, and he does what pleases him. Should we not marvel that what has stunningly pleased God is his own suffering and degradation, the emptying of himself in order to fill salvation's cup?

So what does it mean to imitate that self-sacrificing love?

For one, when Jesus took on his cross, he laid down "fullness"—and it is a sobering example that God has never signed his name to our promissory notes of marriage, children, financial security, meaningful work, and health. If the empty tomb is the sign of a new creation, the cross is the sign of a broken one. "Now that there is a tension between fulfillment and piety should not surprise us in a world distorted by sin, that is, separation from God."[178]Let's not forget that we're still in the middle act of the drama, groaning for God to finally

---

176   Taylor, *A Secular Age*, 651.
177   Ibid., 644.
178   Ibid., 645.

and fully repair this world, which can't help but disappoint. No one gets his best life now. As Elisabeth Eliot writes in her book, *A Path Through Suffering*, "Does our faith rest in having our prayers answered as we think they should be answered, or does it rest on that mighty love that went down into death for us? We can't really tell where it rests, can we, until we're in real trouble."[179]

Further, when Jesus took up his cross, he laid down, in a mysterious way, his freedom. To be clear, the author of Hebrews insists Jesus did not go to the cross against his own will: "Behold, I have come to do your will, O God" (10:7). And yet we have the scene of a kneeling, weeping, pleading Jesus in the Garden of Gethsemane where, in a dramatic reversal of humanity's first act of self-sovereignty, God refused autonomy and chose surrender instead, emptying himself of prerogative and "becoming obedient to the point of death, even death on a cross" (Phil. 2:8). Our ethic is not autonomous freedom, but obedient love. "One central constituent of Christian revelation is that God not only wills our good, a good which includes human flourishing, but was willing to go to extraordinary lengths to ensure this, in the becoming human and the suffering of his son."[180] Like Jesus, we are free to deprive ourselves so another might flourish.

ALLELUIA

The Lord's Prayer teaches us to pray for God's kingdom to come; it also teaches us to pray for daily bread. For all the tension pent up in those seemingly disparate petitions, perhaps

---

179   Elisabeth Elliot, *A Path Through Suffering* (Ann Arbor, MI: Vine, 1990), 65.
180   Taylor, *A Secular Age*, 649.

Bonhoeffer resolves it best in a letter to his friend, Eberhard Bethge: "God, the Eternal, wants to be loved with our whole heart, not to the detriment of earthly love or to diminish it, but as a sort of *cantus firmus*"—the fixed melody line in a polyphonic composition.[181]

In other words, we say yes to God's earth—but never to the detriment of alleluia.

---

181   Wesley Hill, "The Full This-Worldliness of Life," *Books and Culture*, Sept/Oct 2014. http://www.booksandculture.com/articles/2014/sepoct/full-this-worldliness-of-life.html?

11

THE HEALING POWER OF BODILY PRESENCE

BOB CUTILLO

Taking someone's pulse seems a simple gesture. But when I placed my fingers on Mrs. Smith's wrist to feel the rhythm and regularity of her heartbeat, I had no idea her husband would be so impressed. "See, Charlotte, how different this doctor is? He still checks your pulse himself, just like they did in the old days."

Even farther back than the old days of Mr. Smith, feeling the pulse was an essential part of a doctor's exam. From antiquity to the medieval era, rather than the number per minute, the characteristics of a single pulsation were an integral guide to diagnosis and prognosis.[182]

Today, a machine-generated pulse rate is in the chart before I ever see the patient, so there is no need to feel for

---

182   Nima Ghasemzadeh and A. Maziar Zafari, "A Brief Journey into the History of the Arterial Pulse," *Cardiology Research and Practice*, vol. 2011.

it. Or is there? Quite apart from obtaining another piece of data, this family's reaction to my hand on her wrist writes in bold letters across the next chapter in medicine that to lose embodied connections is to endanger the soul of this caring profession.

So why was Charlotte's husband so surprised when I felt her pulse? Living in an increasingly pulseless and fleshless society, he'd learned that the hands-on approach of an earlier "bedside manner" had quietly ceded to a focus on screens and a reliance on numbers. He was experiencing what Charles Taylor has aptly called the "excarnation" of our age.

In light of this revolutionary phenomenon in modern medicine—and with much appreciation for Taylor's concep-tualization—I invite the reader to look through the window of excarnation at our current pursuit of health. What I hope to show in this limited study is the contrast that arises when we counter the effects of excarnation with the implications of the incarnation of Jesus Christ. But before considering the opportunity offered by the biblical vision, we must first explore what Taylor means by excarnation, and then look at some recent evidence of it at work in our world.

EXCARNATION IN OUR SECULAR AGE

Taylor roots the modern development of excarnation in "the exaltation of disengaged reason as the royal road to knowledge." Based on the Enlightenment assumption that we live in an ordered and impersonal universe governed by exceptionless natural laws, our highest understanding comes through objectification or, as Taylor defines it, "grasping the matter studied as something quite independent of us, where we don't need to understand it through our involvement with it, or the meaning it has in our lives." Disengaged thinking allows us to know things from afar. Rising above a particular, narrow, and biased view of things, we come to believe our "view from nowhere" gives us the privileged perspective of an impartial spectator.[183]

Several fragmentations ensue, however, from this elevated view of disengaged reason. First and most obvious is the disengagement of mind and body, with the separated body added to the objectified world around us.

Second, "moving ever farther away from the lived body,"[184] we increasingly separate knowing from experiencing, factoring out "our embodied feeling, our 'gut reaction' in determining what is right."[185] With abstract knowledge of the good increasingly alienated from practice of the good,[186] we learn to accept whatever expert consultants tell us, even though the generalized or marketable information they bring may have no practical value for our local context.

Third, we accept a split between the natural and the supernatural. If by nature the things of this world are ordered by predictable laws amenable to our reason and understanding, then what is supernatural is external, mysterious, and irrational. With God at best a distant architect of a "universe operating by unchanging laws,"[187] the supernatural must break in from the outside, limiting the miraculous to "a kind of punctual hole blown in the regular order of things from the outside."[188] If it happens, it is rare. In fact, as our power over nature grows, these unusual occurrences look more like

---

183   Taylor, *A Secular Age*, 746.
184   Ibid., 741.
185   Ibid., 288.
186   Ibid., 501.
187   Ibid., 270.
188   Ibid., 547–48.

an interruption—if not a threat—to our greatest good, compared to the reliability and effectiveness of what we can do.[189]

RECENT EVIDENCE OF EXCARNATION

Separations of body and mind, of knowing and experiencing, and of nature and supernature yield some troublesome outcomes as they play out in our culture. From the growing carnage produced by the effects of excarnation in health and medicine, let me offer a few examples.

First, in separating mind from body we have come to believe our bodies belong to us, with the freedom to remodel them as we see fit, according to the technical possibilities available and to the extent we can afford it or our insurance covers it. With the boundaries of medical science constantly expanding, we increasingly turn to the health care system to deliver us from the limitations of our bodies. How easily we forget that health cannot be a deliverable commodity, and care cannot come out of a system.[190] With doctors spending twice as much time managing systems as being with patients, the loss of face-to-face time between doctor and patient is one of the major sources of dissatisfaction—for both practitioner and patient—in surveys of health care today.[191]

Second, when knowledge is severed from experience, we allow our bodies to be managed as abstract pieces and parts

---

189   Consider the Legend of the Grand Inquisitor in Dostoyevsky's masterpiece, *The Brothers Karamozov,* as an insightful and disturbing literary example.

190   Ivan Illich, "Brave New Biocracy: Health Care from Womb to Tomb," *New Perspectives Quarterly* 11(1) (1994): 4–12. http://www.davidtinapple.com/illich/1994_biocracy.html

191   Brandi White, David Twiddy, "The State of Family Medicine: 2017," *Family Practice Management* 24 (1) (2017): 26–33.

that should predictably obey the statistical rules of disembodied populations. Many in my profession think it a great success that we have convinced our patients to focus on their numbers. "What is my blood pressure today?" or "How high is my cholesterol and PSA test?" they now ask, assuming good numbers mean good health. But training patients to think their numbers are more important than their experience is a pyrrhic victory for medicine. With doctor and patient alike focused on the interpreted body, neither has time to feel the pulse of the lived body to discover what is really hurting.

Third, believing that our objectified bodies recover from sickness as a predictable result of medical science making use of exceptionless laws, there is no reason to be thankful. In days past we recognized pneumonia could be fatal and recovery from it was cause for gratitude and marvel. Today we see it as simple demonstration of knowledge overcoming a solvable problem. We can still thank God "in the gaps," but our growing control over nature renders that an ever-shrinking space.[192]

Finally, in making our bodies our individual projects, we easily neglect the health of the community we inhabit as if it has nothing to do with our own health.[193] Separated from those around us, each of us pursues personal health apart from our neighbor. Instead of friends whose wellbeing concerns us, we see others as strangers, even enemies in the fight for limited health care. Pitting my needs against yours, it's not surprising our health care debates become partisan struggles for control rather than means of pursuing the common good.

---

192   Taylor, *A Secular Age*, 574.
193   Bob Cutillo. *Pursuing Health in an Anxious Age* (Wheaton, IL: Crossway, 2016), 137–48.

CHALLENGE FOR THE CHURCH

As Taylor reminds us, the "understanding of wholeness which has to include a crucial place for the body is a legacy of our Christian civilization."[194] But for the most part, today's church has been woefully unaware of how deeply the Cartesian split between mind and body has influenced our culture. Forgetting its own historic struggle with the perpetually attractive heresy of Gnosticism, the cleavage between body and soul has opened a fresh fissure running through the heart of today's church.[195]

So with the church largely on the sidelines, and late modernity content to misconstrue or ignore the intimate union of body and soul, the body set afloat has become easy prey to the false ideas of this age. The body has been quickly marginalized to reductive matter, allowing us to believe we can conform it to our own image and overcome its susceptibility to sickness and death.[196] In like manner we have minimized embodied experience, giving priority to abstract and disembodied interactions that reinforce our preference for comfortable distance and an illusion of control. Strikingly absent is the deep Christian conviction of the finite body as gift, given in creation in deep unity with the soul, and formed for embodied relationship with others.

To regain the proper place of the body in human destiny, there is no greater gift than God himself inhabiting

---

194   Taylor, *A Secular Age*, 610.
195   Wendell Berry, "The Body and the Earth," in *The Unsettling of America: Culture and Agriculture* (San Francisco, CA: 1977), 103-12. http://www.presenttruthmag.com/archive/XXX-VIII/38-6.htm
196   Cutillo, *Pursuing Health in an Anxious Age*, 71-95.

fragile flesh and dwelling among us. The incarnation counters every effort at excarnation with the essential nature of embodied life.

Let us look at the good it produces in us, and the effect it may have on others.

THE BODY IN VULNERABLE RELATIONSHIP WITH OTHERS

The excarnation of our age reinforces our natural tendency to minimize the weakness and vulnerability of our bodies, especially as revealed in relationship with others. It's easier to think in theories about people and relate to their disembodied images on screens than to risk the reality of being close and vulnerable to their idiosyncrasies. We even prefer to do charity in programmed and planned ways rather than directly interact with a hurting individual on the road.

But what if our vulnerability in the presence of another is a gift? What if our deepest resources for good can only be discovered in our vulnerable relationship with others? What if our journey toward God is not about Gnostic separation of spirit from world or body from soul but about intimate union and vulnerable interaction with other embodied souls?

In contrast to our natural avoidance, the biblical story is shaped by the contingencies of real life and divine love revealed through the surprise of embodied encounters. If excarnation moves us away from *agape* love, in enfleshed experiences we discover it. As Taylor points out, "Agape moves outward from the guts; the New Testament word for 'taking pity,' *splangnizesthai*, places the response in the bowels."[197] Far from disengaged reason's suspicion, the few instances where this

---

197   Taylor, *A Secular Age*, 741.

"gut reaction" appears in the Gospels show that fully knowing and fully loving can only be found in incarnate experience.

It is instructive to consider the times when Jesus is moved. Sometimes the crowds provoke it, as when he sees them harassed and helpless, like sheep without a shepherd (Matt. 9:36), or when thousands have been with him for days and grow hungry (Matt. 15:32). Another instance surrounds a widow's tears as they carry her only son's body to the grave (Luke 7:11–15). It happens both early in Jesus's ministry as he tries to move on to preach (Mark 1:40–41), and also late on the road to Jerusalem as he stumbles toward the cross (Matt. 20:29–34). Unexpectedly encountering a leper begging for healing or two blind men longing to see, he is stopped in his tracks by their needs. In all these circumstances, Jesus is moved to deep compassion (*splangnizesthai*) that flows from his incarnate involvement with a hurting world.

We also find this heartfelt response in two of Jesus's most well-known parables. In the story of the prodigal son, the father—filled with compassion (*splangnizesthai*) when he sees his wayward son returning—runs to embrace him (Luke 15:20). And in story of the good Samaritan, unlike the priest and the Levite who pass by, the outcast crosses the road to see the hurt man, and "when he saw him, he took pity (*splangnizesthai*) on him" (Luke 10:33). With the words, "Go and do likewise" (Luke 10:37), Jesus makes this gut reaction and the actions that follow a model of how to care for suffering humanity in every age.

But here I must be honest. As I try following Jesus in my own embodied life, my initial "gut reaction" can be anything but caring. When Tommy came to the homeless clinic, I suddenly wished I were anywhere but there. He was 30 years old, coming down off a methamphetamine high, and dirty, disheveled, and smelly from no sleep or shower for several days. Worst of all he looked to me for help—most immediately for

the neglected and infected wounds on his hands from a recent street fight. I turned away aghast at how someone could
abuse his own body, and became angry at his expectations
of me for help. Then I looked at his chart and saw his story.
Sexually abused as a child in foster care by the very people he
should have been able to trust, Tommy was only repeating
the abuse he'd learned from a young age.

In his book *Works of Love*, Danish philosopher Søren Kierkegaard tells a parable of two artists. The first has traveled
and seen countless people in the world, but can find none
worth painting. Each one he sees is imperfect; each one has
faults. The second artist has traveled nowhere, yet in each
person he meets he finds beauty worth painting. The second
artist, Kierkegaard remarks, brings "a certain something"
to each encounter—a view of the other that redefines the
human encounter.[198]

When I turned back to Tommy after his wounds had
been washed and bandaged, I saw something I had not seen
before: a sadness in his eyes as he looked at what he was doing
to himself, and a glimmer of hope that his future could be
different. And at that moment I felt compassion.

THE BODY IN HEALING PRESENCE WITH OTHERS

If we draw near in embodied love, we may be surprised by
the healing power of bodily presence. Many years ago, I was
training in family medicine at Cook County Hospital in Chicago, and began seeing a patient in my clinic named Melvin.
Over the course of two years I came to know Melvin and his
wife well, as she accompanied him on most visits. When I

---

198   Søren Kierkegaard, *Works of Love*, trans. by Howard V. Hong
and Edna H. Hong (New York, NY: Princeton, 1962): 156–57.

diagnosed her husband with inoperable liver cancer, she was there. And the night he died, she called me to come to the house to be with them, as I promised I would.

Watching the first person I attended pass from this life to the next was enough to make the moment memorable. But what I remember most vividly was the funeral. When the service had finished, I was stopped again and again by friends and family, each wanting to thank me for being present when he died. I walked away in wonder at the mystery of what happened that night—that a young doctor, having so little to offer, could be a healer simply because I cared, because I was *there*. I have not stopped plumbing the depths of that mystery ever since.

FOR HEALTH

"From now on we regard no one from a worldly point of view" (2 Cor. 5:16), the apostle writes, because as new creations in Christ we have received the capacity to see others with new eyes. Yet it is a fragile perspective. Ever since Jesus Christ came in the flesh, the spirit of disembodiment has been at work in the world to separate what belongs together—whether body and soul, knowledge and experience, nature and supernature, or you and me.

Though the excarnation of our age presents unique challenges, the basic dilemma of the neighbor on the road still remains the same. We worry with the priest and the Levite, "What will happen to *me* if I go near?" while we wonder with the Samaritan, "What will happen to *him* if I don't?" The surprise of the incarnation is to discover that crossing the road is the path to true health for both of us.

12

THE DISRUPTIVE WITNESS OF ART

ALAN NOBLE

Perhaps the most promising sphere for applying Charles Taylor's ideas in *A Secular Age* is the arts. Here the cross-pressures of the "immanent frame" are keenly felt and, to a lesser extent, relieved through articulations of fullness grounded in our allegories of the transcendent. Taylor's treatment of secularism, cross-pressures, and "subtler languages" can help us better understand the arts and literature and bear witness to God. He offers Christians a more insightful description of modern art and literature by revealing the anxieties and desires that haunt modern people.

But Taylor also gives a promising prescription for how the arts can contribute a "disruptive witness" within the immanent frame. In heeding his words, we can become better participants in and creators of art.

WORLDVIEW SHIFT

Taylor's conception of secularism suggests that evangelicals should shift away from interpreting art primarily through the lens of "worldview" and focus more on the conditions of belief. In works of art and literature, we encounter particular attempts at reckoning with life both within the immanent frame and in light of the pull toward the transcendent—the "cross-pressures" of modernity. The emphasis here is not on the explicit, discrete, and coherent belief system or worldview in a text, because in the secular age belief is fragile, fragmented, and pluralist.[199] Every vision of the good life is contested, and we are hyperaware there is always another option. This does not mean discussing how an author works within a Marxist ideology is always inaccurate or unhelpful. But it should draw our attention to the more visceral aspects of the text—the desires, hopes, longings, and ideals it expresses. Approaching works through predefined categories of worldview may close us off to understanding the artist's particular way of envisioning the cross-pressured experience and perhaps the "malaise of immanence," Taylor's term for the sense that we have lost something with the retreat of transcendence.[200]

Taylor notes three significant challenges for life within the immanent frame, three points of tension that define the cross-pressures. Similar to Peter Berger's arguments for transcendence in *A Rumor of Angels*, Taylor doesn't use these items to falsify materialism, but to point out incongruity. He doesn't deny that these issues can be answered from within the closed immanent frame. But he does believe it is difficult to do so without impoverishment: "[H]ow can one account ... for the power of artistic experience, without speaking in terms of some transcendent being or force which interpellates us?"[201] In a sense, Taylor takes the methods of empiri-

---

199   See discussion of the "Nova Effect" in Smith, *How (Not) to be Secular*, 62.

200   Taylor, *A Secular Age*, 309.

201   Ibid., 597.

cism (how do we make sense of this evidence?) but applies it to our sense of being in the world. And that "sense of being in the world" requires a much more nuanced analysis than "worldview" typically offers us. From a strictly materialist perspective, it is difficult to account for the human capacity for agency, the weightiness of moral obligations, and the spiritual power of beauty "without impoverishment."[202]

BEAUTY IS A PROBLEM

Now, this line of reasoning does not lead to proof of God's existence or the necessity of belief in true transcendence (as opposed to analogies of transcendence, which is the non-theist alternative). But it does tell a better story and offers a more full and satisfying interpretation of existence. And in a culture overwhelmed with contrasting narratives of existence, that counts for something.

Beauty is a problem for modern people—and not one we are prone to ignore. We are fascinated, even obsessed with it. Yet this obsession typically looks like efforts to recast beauty in ways that retain a sense of awe from within the immanent frame. Taylor calls this "immanent transcendence"[203] (interestingly, humanitarianism and social justice work are sometimes the equivalent of this move in the realm of ethics).[204] But I'd like to call them *allegories* of transcendence, in that they are not in any meaningful sense transcendent, but are simply allusions to transcendence.[205] Our culture will con-

---

202   Taylor, *A Secular Age*, 607.
203   Ibid., 726.
204   Ibid., 677.
205   There is an ontological distinction between the transcendence that enters immanence through the incarnation in Christiani-

tinue to produce art that depicts allegories of transcendence, from the green light at the end of the bay in *The Great Gatsby* to the ache of love in Radioheads's "True Love Waits." We will find allegories of transcendence in commercials that promise us things like the end of racial injustice if we only drink the right soda.

The question for evangelicals is how we will respond. The two principal responses are interpretation (analysis and criticism) and creation.

MAKE SENSE OF EXISTENCE

As participants in culture, all Christians are interpreters, and the framework Taylor provides can help us to more accurately and insightfully interpret art. Interpretation never happens in a vacuum. Works of art and literature (I include "pop culture" here as well) are attempts by fallen people to tell some truth about a fallen world created by God. When we interpret these works, then, we are participating in a larger, collective effort to make sense of existence and to make sense of how others make sense of existence. Christians may be tempted to opt out of this work, since they may feel they have "existence" mostly figured out. But this is hubris. There are socioeconomic, technological, geographical, interpersonal, and cultural forces that shape our experience of being, and when we participate in great cultural works, we gain a kind of wisdom.

This participation almost always happens in community. When we watch a film, we immediately want to discuss it.

---

ty and the immanent-transcendence of modernity that always remains ontologically immanent but in some sense *feels*, or *looks*, or *approximates* transcendence through vastness.

We share our musical experiences. We have book clubs. We interpret together. Once we see this desire for shared experience, Taylor's project becomes invaluable, since it allows us to more clearly see the tensions that haunt our times.

When we can look at Jay Gatsby's desire for Daisy Buchannan as not merely an intense romantic desire but a doomed allegory of transcendence, one that (nearly-century-old spoiler) *kills* him, we have a new way to speak to our neighbors about the human heart, the contemporary world, and God. We can make explicit the cross-pressures that haunt us, and consider how certain narratives fail or succeed in accounting for our agency, ethics, or beauty without impoverishment.

In the case of *The Great Gatsby*, F. Scott Fitzgerald depicts Daisy's failure as an object of transcendence (as Ernest Becker would say, she could not bear the burden of godhood, nor could any mortal).[206] Yet the depiction of Gatsby's longing for some ideal outside of the immanent frame is compelling to readers precisely because it is so relatable. Part of the pleasure of the text is in sympathizing with Gatsby's longing and suffering. When we use Taylor's language to interpret art and literature in this way, it allows us to better understand both our neighbors and ourselves.

Please don't misunderstand this approach as a New Evangelism Method. It's not. It is, however, a way to bear witness to God's truth in a highly contested world. Part of what makes interpreting works in this way so moving is that Christians can empathize with a horizontal longing for transcendence even though we have a robust belief in a transcendent

---

206 Ernest Becker, *The Denial of Death* (New York, NY: Free Press, 1973), 166.

God. This is because, as Taylor notes, we are *all* living in the immanent frame. While we may be open to transcendence, there is a sense in which we have to labor to pursue it. Practically, this means Gatsby's desire for total existential justification through a romantic relationship is not a foreign feeling for Christians. We know this desire, or something very much like it. And in the act of participating in these cultural works that offer allegories of transcendence or even hints at true transcendence, we can praise what is true as we point to what is more fully true. The longing we experience is a longing we *share* with our unbelieving neighbors. Which means that when we share our interpretations, we are doing so from a place of common experience, not disengaged superiority.

ALTERNATIVE IMAGINARY

For most of us, Taylor's story of secularism, cross-pressures, and the immanent frame will be most helpful in interpreting cultural works. But for a few, there is a more pressing and, I think, exciting application of Taylor's ideas. Near the end of *A Secular Age*, he suggests literature (and I would argue the other arts as well) may offer one of the most poignant, disruptive voices for our times.[207] Taylor's account of unbelief in the 21st century suggests that it is not typically *intellectual* objections that keep people from faith, but the *visceral* pull of the immanent frame in the background. So we need to offer an alternative social imaginary, one that conceives of human fullness in Christ. It may require the creation of a "new language or literary style," but the Christian artist may depict

---

207   Taylor, *A Secular Age*, 732.

transcendence from within immanence in a way that speaks to the lived experience of modern people.[208]

For his model, Taylor cites Flannery O'Connor.[209] Evangelicals' general admiration for O'Connor may blind us to Taylor's point here, so I think it is instructive to look at the particular ways O'Connor works from within the immanent frame to push against closed immanence. Taylor notes how she told stories grounded in the everyday, worldly experience of the immanent frame while providing "a point not visible to the naked eye," a point that forces a paradigm shift.[210] One thinks of the grandmother's epiphany at the end of "A Good Man Is Hard to Find" as an example. She embodies the petty evil of selfishness, perfectly absorbed in her own world and desires. Yet her epiphany at the end of the Misfit's gun points to a force of transformation from outside herself, a force of grace.

Taylor doesn't want us to see O'Connor's use of violence and the grotesque as the only or primary way writers can offer signs of transcendence in an immanently framed world, but she does offer *a* model. Good contemporary art and literature will convey these cross-pressures. But the Christian artist may tilt toward the plausibility of true transcendence, demonstrating how this "take" on existence deeply satisfies since it doesn't result in an impoverished vision.

---

208 Taylor, *A Secular Age*, 732.
209 Ibid.
210 O'Connor quoted in Taylor, *A Secular Age*, 732.

HARD BALANCE

The opportunity for the Christian artist to point a way out of a closed immanent frame ought to be a source of both inspiration for artists and support from their communities. But it is hard to strike the balance Taylor is calling for, especially in a manner that can be effectively received. Art that unironically depicts the transcendent, as opposed to an allegory of transcendence, will tend to upset audiences. The ending of Graham Greene's *The End of the Affair* is a good example. Greene's novel recounts a love affair and a conversion to Catholicism during the Battle of Britain. Although God and Catholicism are themes within the text, the world of the novel—the characters, the events, the drama—takes place comfortably within an immanent frame, until the conclusion.

The novel's final sections introduce a series of miracles. Though most have a plausibly natural explanation, it requires the reader to accept a high degree of coincidence. But the last miracle—the clearing of one character's birthmark—has no other explanation. Critics and readers have been troubled by this miracle in an otherwise sensible novel.[211] It strains credulity. It forces the reader to accept a particular account of the transcendent, rather than leaving it open. Interestingly enough, the protagonist rejects the miracle as evidence of God, demonstrating that Greene is sensitive to the difficulty of imagining something beyond the immanent. Yet despite acknowledging how hard it would be to accept a miracle while living within an immanent frame, and despite Greene's

---

211   See: Harvey Curtis Webster, *Graham Greene: Some Critical Considerations* (Lexington, KY: University of Kentucky Press, 1967), 22.

beautiful prose and storytelling, for some the novel's conclusion remains an aesthetic failure.

I don't tell this story to discourage artists from following Taylor's advice, but simply to show that it is no easy task. The temptation on one side will be to misrepresent the immanent frame—to cast it as wholly unsatisfying or joyless, when the truth is many live relatively pleasant lives without recourse to faith or any form of transcendence. If anything, technology and consumerism have made it easier than ever to live a fairly pleasant, distracted life within the immanent frame. Likewise, we may try to exaggerate the experience of an encounter with transcendence such that the audience feels unable to empathize. The key, I suspect, is the reality that we've almost all experienced the force of the immanent frame and a longing for something beyond it—and so the audience has the ability to empathize with both pulls. Artists can work with these foundational experiences, so long as they don't abuse them through contrivance or unearned emotions.

SIGNIFICANT INVESTMENT

Bearing witness to the Christian faith in the 21st century requires a disruptive witness,[212] one that unsettles our neighbor's assumptions about life within the immanent frame. One of the most powerful ways to accomplish this is through interpreting and creating cultural works that speak not only to our minds but also our bodies, emotions, and memories. Taylor has given us valuable tools to better understand our neighbors and the kinds of anxieties that haunt both them

---

212   For more on this concept, see Alan Noble, *Disruptive Witness: Speaking Truth in a Distracted Age* (Downers Grove, IL: IVP, forthcoming).

and ourselves. To cultivate the deep knowledge to apply Taylor's ideas, we will need significant investment in the Christian liberal and creative arts.

When evangelicals think about their relationship to the broader culture, I see two prominent approaches. The first is to treat their faith as just another aspect of their identity. In this trend, Christians conceive of themselves *first* as modern American individuals. The kinds of movies, films, songs, books, and video games they consume—and the way they interpret those works—is largely indistinct from their nonbelieving neighbors, except that they may have less tolerance for sex scenes, blasphemy, and excessive violence. The second approach sees the culture as divided into worldview categories, with each worldview vying for power and insidiously persuading us through the media. In this trend, the kinds of cultural works Christians consume and the way they interpret them tend to be distinct from their nonbelieving neighbors—so distinct that they may find it difficult to converse about the same film in any meaningful way. In light of Taylor's work, it seems both of these popular approaches are misguided, since they fail to account for the force of the immanent frame and the cross-pressures we experience within it.

Charles Taylor's work invites us to a much more complex—but much more insightful—conception of culture and our relationship to it. He emphasizes the way a basic human desire for fullness, which tends to be oriented toward some kind of transcendent end, motivates cultural works. To pursue this approach, we need foundational investment in Christian liberal arts universities, creative writing and film programs, literary publications, and more. Taylor has done the great service of making us aware of the power of aesthetic witnesses to God's existence and goodness in a society largely held captive by the immanent frame. We are capable of casting an alternative social imaginary, one that disrupts our neighbors' conception of the world by revealing and validating eternity hidden in their hearts (Eccl. 3:11). But to learn to interpret and create cultural works in this way will require time, investment, and mentorship.

13

PIERCING THE IMMANENT FRAME WITH AN ULTRALIGHT BEAM: KANYE AND CHARLES TAYLOR

MIKE COSPER

It's February 13, 2016. Kanye West takes the stage as the musical guest on *Saturday Night Live*. He stands in all-white camoflage, flanked by a choir. Behind them is an angled projection screen scrolling pixelated images of what appears to be clouds. A track starts playing—the voice of a little girl praying, casting out demons ("We don't want no devils in the house"), speaking in tongues. Kanye sings, "We on an ultralight beam, we on an ultralight beam, this is a God dream, this is a God dream, this is everything." His voice is contorted by an auto-tuning effect, simultaneously making it more perfectly in tune and yet more broken, unnatural.

The track is deconstructed and minimalist. No real drumbeat, just occasional stabs and throbs. Kanye prays for serenity, peace, and love. "Lord knows we need it." The choir moves in choppy unison. They join him, singing, "This is an ultralight beam." Two Gospel singers join him, lamenting, "I'm trying to keep my faith . . . why send depression not blessings?"

"I look to the light," one sings. "I know you'll take good care of your child."

Out of the wings comes Chance the Rapper, who before this performance wasn't a household name. He sings, "When they come for you, I will feel your pain. I will field their questions. I will feel your pain. No one can judge."

Suddenly Chance breaks out in verse, his rhymes moving in a fast counter-rhythm to the song's lurching slow one. His first line: "Foot on Devil's neck 'til it drifted Pangea." It is apocalyptic; like an image from John's revelation, stomping on the Devil so hard it causes continental drift. The verse is expressionist—a series of images, phrases, and ideas, all invoking spiritual warfare, fighting demons, seeking freedom.

"You can feel the lyrics, Spirit coming in braille / Tubman in the underground come and follow the trail. I made Sunday Candy I'm never going to hell. I met Kanye West I'm never going to fail." The beat intensifies, the choir dances, the verse comes to its climax. "This is my part; nobody else speak / This is my part; nobody else speak / this little light of mine / glory be to God."

The beat intensifies even more. Chance leaps and shouts, "I'm just having fun with it / you know that a n***** was lost / I laugh in my head cuz my ex lookin' back like a pillar of salt / but people just please don't forget about Jason

Van Dyke[213] / you cannot mess with the light / just look at lil' Chano from 79."[214]

The chorus returns. "I'm trying to keep my faith / but I'm looking for more / somewhere I can feel safe / and end this holy war." Kanye walks to the middle of the stage and falls prostrate. Kirk Franklin emerges from the wings and prays, "Father, this prayer's for everybody who feels like giving up. This prayer's for everybody who feels like they're not good enough. Everybody that said, 'I'm sorry' too many times. Jesus, that's why I'm glad you came to give us eternal life. I'm so glad about it."

The choir erupts, and in a call and response, they join Franklin and sing, "Faith. (In this world we've been looking for) more. (Lord, please keep my little brother) safe. (We stand here and we fight in this) war."

The whole performance is stunning. It's earnest. It seesaws between desperation and celebration. When the song ends, Kanye bursts up from the ground to announce his record is releasing then and there, streaming on the music service Tidal. It breaks the tension of the moment—the deep sense of transcendence—and yanks us back into the present. This is a TV performance, not the desperate pleas of a broken man.

Worse than that, it is (to borrow a phrase from *A Christmas Story*) a crummy commercial.

---

213   He's invoking police shootings. Jason Van Dyke, a Chicago police officer, shot Laquan McDonald, a 17-year-old armed with a small knife. Van Dyke shot him 16 times from 10 feet away. See more: http://www.chicagotribune.com/news/laquan-mcdonald/ct-graphics-laquan-mcdonald-officers-fired-time-line-htmlstory.html

214   One of Chance's names for himself.

BUFFERED SELF

I can think of no other moment from pop culture that so perfectly provides fodder for talking about Taylor's *A Secular Age*. It's all there: the buffered self, the immanent frame, the malaise of immanence, longing for fullness.

Let's start with the buffered self.

Taylor says that pre-modern humanity understood itself as "porous." By this, he means humanity believed their bodies and souls were vulnerable to unseen, external, and spiritual influences:

> This porousness is most clearly in evidence in the fear of possession. Demons can take us over. And indeed, five centuries ago, many of the more spectacular manifestations of mental illness, what we would class as psychotic behavior, were laid at the door of possession, as in the New Testament times.[215]

Porousness wasn't just a negative concept. The good things in our lives and in our minds are also open to external influences:

> Say someone falls in love. . . . An "internal" event, we [meaning, us—moderns] think, albeit susceptible to pressures from the outside. . . .
>
> But now let's say that we see this whole side of life as under the aegis of a goddess, Aphrodite. That means that its going well if it's being smiled on by Aphrodite. This means not only that she is keeping external dan-

---

215   Taylor, *A Secular Age*, 35.

gers at bay; like a human patron, she is in this aspect
causally responsible for the conditions being propitious.
It also means that the blooming of the right internal
motivation is a gift from her. In other words, my being
in the highest motivational condition [I think he means
to say "in love"] is not just a fact about my inner realm
of desires; it is my being the recipient of the gift of the
goddess. The highest condition can't just be placed
unambiguously within; it is placed in that interspace,
where the gift is received.

In other words, pre-modern humanity saw the life of the
mind as subject to external, spiritual, and mysterious influences. Just as madness might exist because of the influence
of evil spirits, love might exist because of the influence of benevolent spirits. Love does not just happen within the mind;
love is something external that penetrates my mind, and I
participate in it. I am vulnerable to love, just as I am vulnerable to madness.

In modern humanity, things are quite different. No
longer is there a plausible sense that our lives are under the
influence of unseen—whether malevolent or benevolent—
spiritual forces. Instead, there are clear, palpable explanations
for life's questions. Love evolved to motivate the perpetuation
of the species. Disease comes not from demons, but germs.
Our psychological disorders result either from bad genes or
bad upbringing. This modern way of understanding feels safer
(and thus "buffered") because our problems are comprehensible, and not the product of mysterious forces:

See the contrast. A modern is feeling depressed, melancholy. He is told: it's just your body chemistry,
you're hungry, or there is a hormone malfunction, or
whatever. Straightaway, he feels relieved. He can take a

distance from this feeling, which is ipso facto declared not justified. Things don't really have this meaning; it just feels this way, which is the result of a causal action utterly unrelated to the meanings of things. This step of disengagement depends on our modern mind/body distinction, and the relegation of the physical to being "just" a contingent cause of the psychic. But a pre-modern may not be helped by learning that his mood comes from black bile. Because this doesn't permit a distancing. Black bile is melancholy. Now he just knows that he's in the grips of the real thing. Here is the contrast between the modern, bounded self—I want to say "buffered" self and the "porous" self of the earlier enchanted world.[216]

The modern self is "buffered"—safe from the mysteries of an unknowable world. But there are consequences to that buffering. The flip side of being buffered from unknown spiritual powers is that you're cut off—or at least hindered—from any experience of transcendence. Taylor describes our world, where there are explanations for every phenomenon, as the "immanent frame."

Imagine it like a dome. Everything inside the dome is the realm of immanence; outside is the realm of transcendence. People whose imaginations are formed by life in a secular age bump their heads on the ceiling of the dome when they veer near ideas that invoke transcendence, be they religious, moral, or aesthetic.

Taylor says "we come to understand our lives as taking place within a self-sufficient immanent order," and this is the only world we can take seriously. It is made up of things we can touch, taste, smell, and measure, and it is dismissive of

---

216   Taylor, *A Secular Age*, 37–38.

the speculative realm that lies outside of it. "This frame," he writes, " constitutes a 'natural' order, to be contrasted to a 'supernatural' one, an 'immanent' world, over against a possible 'transcendent' one."[217]

MEN IN A CAVE

In her essay "Tradition and the Modern Age," Hannah Arendt makes her own attempt to describe how we've found ourselves in a culture without transcendent categories. According to her account, one can trace it back to the philosophy of Karl Marx, who sought to turn philosophy on its head. She describes Marx's accomplishment through the lens of Plato's cave analogy.

Plato imagined humanity like men shackled in a cave, forced only to know a world of shadows cast on the wall. He wanted to release man from his shackles and move him out of the world of shadows (the realm of immanence) and into the light (the realm of transcendence). Marx wanted the opposite. Away with your transcendence; let's deal with reality: politics and economics. Arendt writes, "Turning the tradition upside down within its own framework, [Marx] did not actually get rid of Plato's ideas, though he did record the darkening of the clear sky where those ideas, as well as many other presences, had once become visible to the eyes of men."[218]

In other words, in a secular age, we've returned to the cave, to shackles, to a world of shadows.

Herein lies the curse of secularism. Ecclesiastes 3:11 says God has put eternity in the hearts of men. The im-

---

217   Taylor, *A Secular Age*, 542.
218   Hannah Arendt, *Between Past and Future* (New York, NY: Penguin, 2006), 40.

manent frame is ultimately a dissatisfying place to live, because it shackles the human heart inside a world that is simply too small for it. Our longing for transcendence can't be squelched, nor can it be satisfied. And, as James K. A. Smith puts it (summarizing Taylor), "The dissatisfaction and emptiness can propel a return to transcendence. But often—perhaps more often than not now?—the 'cure' to this nagging pressure of absence is *within immanence*, and it is this quest that generates the nova effect, looking for love/meaning/significance/quasi 'transcendence' *within* the immanent order."[219]

This leads to a search for satisfaction in other ways: through consumption, pleasure, or a certain kind of tribalism, all of which have a way of temporarily distracting us from our longing for eternity. A malaise sets in, which Taylor says is one of a secular age's most notable characteristics.

He identifies three specific kinds of malaise:

> (1) the sense of the fragility of meaning, the search for an overarching significance; (2) the felt flatness of our attempts to solemnize the crucial moments of passage in our lives; and (3) the utter flatness, emptiness of the ordinary.[220]

To expand these slightly: (1) We long for an overarching account of the meaning of life, our purpose here on earth. (2) We don't know what to do with life's big moments—weddings, childbirth, funerals, and so on—because our secularist account for them is inadequate for the deeper sense of meaning we *intuit* about them. (3) Daily life always feels like something is missing.

---

219 Smith, *How (Not) to Be Secular*, 69.
220 Taylor, *A Secular Age*, 309.

On this third point, Taylor writes:

[W]e can also just feel the lack in the everyday. This can
be where it most hurts. This seems to be felt particular-
ly by people of some leisure and culture. For instance,
some people sense a terrible flatness in the everyday,
and this experience has been identified particularly with
commercial, industrial, or consumer society. They feel
emptiness of the repeated, accelerating cycle of desire
and fulfillment in consumer culture; the cardboard
quality of bright supermarkets, or neat row housing in
a clean suburb; the ugliness of slag heaps, or an aging
industrial townscape.[221]

Those who become frustrated with the malaise of the city
move to the suburbs, only to find the same emptiness and
flatness there. To quote Woody Allen, "It turns out life is just
a little unsatisfying."

But there are nonetheless moments, within the overarching feeling of malaise, when something opens up in the
immanent frame and a little light gets in. Taylor uses the
word "fullness" to describe these moments—moments of
transcendence that feel too big to make sense of within the
secular frame. It is the kind of life we all aspire to—a sense of
completeness and wholeness.

It is also something artists experience in their work. Brian Koppelman is a filmmaker and screenwriter. He's also an
atheist. In an interview with singer/songwriter Glen Phillips,
he admitted, "For an atheist, these moments are very confus-

---

221   Taylor, *A Secular Age*, 309.

ing."[222] This is precisely the experience of fullness. Something a little too big to account for in immanent terms.

CROSS-PRESSURED LIFE

Which brings us back to Kanye.

Kanye's work is a clear illustration of the cross-pressured life. His music has demonstrated a struggle with faith from his early beginnings, like in "Jesus Walks." The song begins by describing the life of a drug dealer, wrestling with guilt over his sins and hoping the Devil doesn't break him down. By the end, there's almost a conversion. He *needs* Jesus, and he's testifying to "hustlers, killers, murderers, drug dealers, even strippers." He needs Jesus "the way Kathy needs Regis."

Faith is a central feature of Kanye's music. Sometimes it is angry, bordering on imprecatory prayer, like in "Black Skinhead" from 2013's *Yeezus*. Sometimes he nods to it quietly while he raps graphically about sex, power, and money. But "Ultralight Beam" seems to be the most honest and confessional work of faith in his whole catalogue.

From the beginning of the song, Kanye exposes the haunted fear that his soul might indeed be porous. "We don't want no devils in this house," says a little girl's voice. "We want the Lord." It is a prayer of both exorcism and invocation. It is as if he's *haunted* by faith—a word Taylor uses to describe life in a secular age. Haunted by the dream that perhaps there's something more.

---

222   Brian Koppelman, interview with Glen Phillips from *The Moment with Brian* Koppelman, podcast audio, 9/6/2016. http://www.slate.com/articles/podcasts/the_moment/2016/09/glen_phillips_of_toad_the_wet_sprocket_talks_about_being_swallowed_by_the.html

Because make no mistake, in the rest of Kanye's life, he's unapologetically looking for meaning within immanence. He's married to Kim Kardashian, one of the most famous, wealthy, and pampered human beings on earth. He's regularly bragging about his greatness on Twitter and on camera. His other songs boast about sex with models, seducing record executive's wives, and varied expressions of power and wealth. Kanye is *not* a Christian role model.

That's what makes "Ultralight Beam" so telling. All the pleasures of life in immanence leave him unsatisfied. "I'm trying to keep my faith / but I'm looking for more / somewhere I can feel safe / and end this holy war." His buffered self feels fragile and porous. His search within immanence has left him wanting. So he surrounds himself with his own "cloud of witnesses"—Kelly Price, The-Dream, Chance the Rapper, and Kirk Franklin—who offer something akin to intercessory prayers.

Witnesses might be the best word to describe these collaborators, since most of their work is far more overtly religious than Kanye's. Franklin, for instance, is a giant in the world of Gospel music, and has put faith at the center of his work. Chance, too, is a much more consistently Christian voice. It is hard to imagine Kanye writing "How Great Is Our God," Chance's song that begins with three minutes of an a cappella choir singing Chris Tomlin's praise-and-worship hit of the same name.

Kanye can't seem to make peace with the world of faith, can't make sense of it. What does make sense to Kanye is the world of immanence. He gives that away at the end of the *Saturday Night Live* performance, when he manically leaps to his feet to announce the release of his record. The performance is drama; the sales and distribution of the album is real. Likewise, on the album *The Life of Pablo*, "Ultralight Beam" is the opener; the next song, "Father Stretch My

Hands, Pt. 1," opens with a vulgar description of sex. It is as though Kanye reaches for repentance and transcendence and immediately returns to the world of immanent pleasure. He repents in the wrong direction.

This is the pendulum of Kanye's music: movements toward religious hope followed by despair and indulgence.

Yet there's another element of "Ultralight Beam" that resonates nicely with Taylor's ideas. Taylor speaks specifically about the poetry of Gerard Manley Hopkins (who, we should note, is a very different poet than Kanye West). "Poetry is potentially world-making," Taylor says.[223] It creates new symbols and provides new meaning. It can create a kind of breach in the immanent frame, opening our imaginations to the possibility of something *more*. Something transcendent.

I think this is true of the arts in general. Literature like that of David Foster Wallace or John Jeremiah Sullivan has a way of probing and poking holes in the limits of the immanent frame. Damien Hirst, a visual artist, takes objects from the real world (embalmed cattle, or an embalmed great white shark) and presents them to us in a way that is undeniably transcendent and haunting. The point being, the immanent frame isn't made of concrete.

There's a scene in the original *Jurassic Park* where they're touring past the velociraptors' cages. Robert Muldoon, the game warden, notes that they used to attack the fences when the feeders came. Systematically striking various sections. "They were testing them for weaknesses," the game warden says.

This, I think, is what the arts can do in a secular age. They can test and probe the immanent frame, looking for weaknesses. James K. A. Smith gets at this when, summa-

---

223   Taylor, *A Secular Age*, 756.

rizing Taylor, he writes: "Don't you *feel* it? Don't you have those moments of either foreboding or on-the-cusp ela- tion where you can't shake the sense that there must be something *more*?"[224]

This is Kanye's explicit cry in "Ultralight Beam." In a secular age, we grasp for concrete reasons why art "works"— how it evokes activity in the brain, the neurosystem, and the body that accounts for the feeling we get when we encounter it. The best artists push those accounts to their limits, and make us question whether they're sufficient to describe what the artwork has done to us. They push us to the edge of the immanent frame.

"I'm looking for more," Kanye says. And the opportunity for the church in a secular age is to greet that thought with joy. Because there is so much more.

---

224   Smith, *How (Not) to Be Secular*, 137.

THE GOSPEL COALITION

THE GOSPEL COALITION is a fellowship of evangelical churches deeply committed to renewing our faith in the gospel of Christ and to reforming our ministry practices to conform fully to the Scriptures. We have committed ourselves to invigorating churches with new hope and compelling joy based on the promises received by grace alone through faith alone in Christ alone.

We desire to champion the gospel with clarity, compassion, courage, and joy—gladly linking hearts with fellow believers across denominational, ethnic, and class lines. We yearn to work with all who, in addition to embracing our confession and theological vision for ministry, seek the lordship of Christ over the whole of life with unabashed hope in the power of the Holy Spirit to transform individuals, communities, and cultures.

Join the cause and visit *TGC.org* for fresh resources that will equip you to love God with all your heart, soul, mind, and strength, and to love your neighbor as yourself.

TGC.ORG

Made in the USA
Middletown, DE
25 September 2017